D1027195

MSDR: Medical Sales Desk Reference

Increase Your Sales and Commissions then Fast Track your Career as a Modern Medical or Pharmaceutical Sales Executive

By

Vendesi Group & Ryan Gray

authorHOUSE™

1663 LIBERTY DRIVE, SUITE 200
BLOOMINGTON, INDIANA 47403
(800) 839-8640
WWW.AUTHORHOUSE.COM

This book is a work of non-fiction. Unless otherwise noted, the author and the publisher make no explicit guarantees as to the accuracy of the information contained in this book and in some cases, names of people and places have been altered to protect their privacy.

© 2005 Vendesi Group & Ryan Gray. All Rights Reserved.

All rights reserved. No part of this book or any attachments, special reports, cd-roms, videos, audio presentations, spreadsheets, hyperlinks or files may be reproduced or transmitted in any form or by any means, electronic or mechanical, including photocopying, recording, or by any information storage and retrieval system, without permission in writing from Vendesi Group, LLC.

First published by AuthorHouse 04/14/05

ISBN: 1-4208-4011-8 (sc)

Printed in the United States of America
Bloomington, Indiana

This book is printed on acid-free paper.

Design by Vendesi Group, LLC.
MSDR: Medical Sales Desk Reference™ is a fully owned subsidiary of Vendesi Group, LLC.

Contents

Introduction

About us

The medical sales professionals at Vendesi Group are excited to offer you proven ideas and systems covering specific aspects of our field under the Medical Sales Desk Reference umbrella. Created by founder Ryan Gray, we are the industry leaders in providing intellectual property to medical sales representatives in the field and the corporations they represent. Individuals purchase our content to assist them in reaching various goals pertaining to medical sales. We partner with multinational corporations by producing and distributing the industry exclusive MSDR: Medical Sales Desk Reference™ – Corporate Edition.

Our data is gathered from our combined experiences selling to doctors and hospitals since the late 1960s. When you include the team of advisors who contributed to this project, the experience we share with you represents over 100 years in medical sales, sales management and marketing expertise!

Jack Erickson, our most tenured member, spent 29 years in management with different divisions of Johnson & Johnson. There are literally hundreds of sales representatives who owe their careers to Jack. He is one who has truly seen and done it all. He retired in 1995 among the most award-winning managers in the history of J&J. He was a great leader and mentor. Many of the medical professionals at Vendesi Group worked for Jack at some time in their careers. We are excited to have him on our team.

Many other people are responsible for the quality of this work. Vendesi Group requested and received wonderful feedback from our family of friends in the industry. For all their contributions, we say thank you. This group worked for some of the best companies in the world. Some of those companies are:

Guidant, CRM

Ethicon

Johnson & Johnson Medical

Critikon

Merck

C.R. Bard

De Puy Orthopedics

Cordis Cardiology

St. Jude Medical

Medtronic

Advanced Cardiovascular Solutions

Abbott Labs

Stryker

Jelco Labs

Daig

vendesigroup.com

We invite you to visit our website at www.vendesigroup.com for the most updated medical selling information available.

There is no better way to share critical, timely and evolving information with you than on our website. The purpose of this written material is to share with you the proven methods for success in medical sales. These core concepts do not change over time. For those things that do change (like new selling tips), we (and you) need to be able to communicate more rapidly. The web is the only place to do this.

While you are visiting, sign yourself and your team up for our weekly electronic newsletter. We remove the clutter of most E-Zines by sending you a concise newsletter filled with ideas to put money in your pocket.

Are you interested in contributing an idea for the weekly newsletter? Contact us through the website. If we use your idea, you will be paid a modest fee and you can add the publication experience to your résumé or personal accomplishment portfolio. Being published on any level is a great accomplishment and shows your expertise in the field.

About our information

Here is a quick overview of all the products from Vendesi Group:

MSDR: Medical Sales Desk Reference™ Series:
Guide to Finding Your Medical or Pharmaceutical Sales Job

This material explains the proper way you get into the medical or pharmaceutical sales business. We use our combined experience in the field to teach you exactly what you need to know to get into the business. We demonstrate ways of gaining medical *experiences* to make your résumé sizzle. We also give suggestions on talking about *those* things during your interviews as well as how to close like a professional. We sum things up with unique ideas to get your message out to potential companies.

Vendesi Group has a sincere interest in seeing you reach your goal of obtaining a medical sales job. Our desire is for you to choose Vendesi Group as your medical sales coach throughout your career. If we bring value to you with this guide, you will likely join our other successful clients by purchasing the *MSDR: Personal Edition* and eventually our *MSDR: Guide to the ULTRA Medical Companies*. Your success in gaining access to this industry is critical to our future! We want you to have the best.

The MSDR: Medical Sales Desk Reference™ - *Personal Edition*

Increase your commissions by 20 percent in 12 months – <u>Guaranteed</u> And Inside information to get promotion after promotion!

This section details insider information to help one already in the field to soar to the top of the company. Become your company's <u>biggest star</u> by learning new and unique strategies to grow your business and your income.

We discuss tactical ideas from super producers to dramatically increase your sales. Our goal is to increase our customers' territory revenue by 20 percent at a minimum and raise their commissions by that figure as well. Included in this section are the best ideas and concepts from the partners at Vendesi Group. If you are not completely satisfied for any reason, we will refund the purchase price of this material. If you will use them, we guarantee they will raise your territory revenue and commissions!

We have also included a $1,000,000 ideas segment with over 20 actionable items. Each one has the potential to individually increase your sales volume $1,000,000 in a single year! Many $100,000 ideas are thrown in as well. Depending on your business structure, one of these ideas can easily create $1,000,000 in increased sales, sometimes in a matter of months. We have seen it happen (so it is possible), and it happens every day!

There are numerable other concepts covered in this section. Some include selling to the medical community and tricks for getting in front of doctors, nurses and key decision makers. A few reps know these ideas exist, but even fewer actually use them. We will wager this is the first time you will see most of these super tactics.

As another teaser, let us ask you the following. Have you ever noticed some people in your organization have "Golden Halos?" Those with the halo absolutely fly up the corporate ladder faster than anyone! They are in a sales position for a brief period, then off to management, then on to other bigger projects and greater responsibilities. There are undiscovered secrets to this upward movement we are going to share with you in this section! Their tricks will be revealed and you can use them to propel YOUR career.

The MSDR: *Medical Sales Desk Reference*™ – *Corporate Edition*

In the MSDR: *Medical Sales Desk Reference*™ – *Corporate Edition,* we took the best information from each section and combined it into one ultimate selling manual for the medical industry. Many medical companies have used standard selling tactics and strategies and tried to apply them to medical sales. No one ever created materials specifically designed for the intricacies of selling to the medical community.

UNTIL NOW

The MSDR: *Medical Sales Desk Reference*™ - *Corporate Edition* adds more than <u>20</u> actionable ideas to our "Ideas to create $1,000,000 in sales" section, bringing the total to over 40. Included are discussions about:

The most powerful sales question

Hosting effective dinner programs

Rewarding your best clients

How to protect key territory information

What does it mean if a customer tells you a competitor's bid?

Should you carry marketing pieces in your car?

And much, much more

We offer group purchase rates for the MSDR as well. Please contact us at www.vendesigroup.com for more details.

About you

"The world has the habit of making room for the man whose actions show that he knows where he is going".

—Napoleon Hill

<u>Vendesi Group</u> wants you to be successful! We are committed to helping you eliminate common mistakes, create more sales and earn a personal fortune in medical sales!

We believe in life that most, if not all, mistakes we could make have already been made by others. Our most difficult assignment is finding this information **before** we make the mistakes! This saves our most valuable resource...time. Fortunately for you, in the field of pharmaceutical and medical sales, our partners lived the good decisions and the bad ones. We then collected the information in the material you now have. We <u>will</u> put you on the express lane to unlimited potential in the medical industry.

Here is a fun story with a great point we would like to share.

The Purple Worm Story

An old man was fishing a new lake with a longtime friend. Because they wanted a successful trip, they hired a professional guide. On the way to the lake, they stopped at a gas station to buy supplies. As he usually did with everyone he met, the old man struck up a conversation with the storekeeper, mentioning their plans for the day. The storekeeper said the old man only needed one thing for fishing success – a bag of purple worms.

The old man bought the worms. His friend and the guide laughed at the purchase.

As their guide steered them to their final destination on the lake, the old man feverishly tied a purple worm to his line. The instant the boat stopped, he started fishing. His friend and the guide made fun of his purple worms and both started fishing with the guide's choice of live bait.

Boom…boom…boom. The old man caught three fish on purple worms while the lines of his friend and the guide lay still.

Eventually, the old man's friend tried a purple worm, but the guide scoffed and continued to use live bait.

Boom…boom…boom… Three more fish landed by the two amateurs — none for the professional guide!

Eventually, the exasperated guide turned and yelled, "Give me one of those @%^#$%^ purple worms!"

Moral of the story: If you find a system that works, duplicate that system first. There will always be time to explore new ideas after you have fish in the boat.

A final important note

It should be added that money or success for its own sake is ultimately empty. Vendesi Group is committed to improving the lives of others. We donate 5 percent of our gross (not net) revenue from the purchase of any product sold to individuals or corporations to these charities. In fact, *our customers choose which charity their 5 percent goes to*. At the time of publishing, those choices include:

- The Alzheimer's Association
- Angel Flight America
- Bear Necessities – Pediatric Cancer Foundation
- CNJ Kenya Medical Mission
- Cystic Fibrosis Foundation
- The Free Wheel Chair Mission
- Freedom Alliance

Others are also included, please see vendesigroup. com for more information on our charities.

The MSDR:
Medical Sales Desk
Reference™©
Corporate Edition
By
Vendesi Group
&
Ryan Gray

Welcome

Welcome to those of you in the medical sales business. The purpose of this material is to make you a star at your company, increase your territory sales and ultimately your commissions. If you utilize the following concepts, new and exciting options will come your way!

Our first order of business is to work with you and develop a plan to increase your paycheck! We have collected the best information from our partners and compiled them into this material. Using these ideas properly and tracking your success, you will add at least 20 percent to your total territory revenue in only 12 months. Such success will not only put money in your pocket, but it will put your career on the fast track of your company.

Speaking of the fast track, we also outline how you can blitz through your organization as only an insider can. Earlier we mentioned how your co-workers with the Golden Halo fly upwards through the corporation faster than anyone. They are in a sales position for a brief period, then off to management, then on to other bigger projects. You know who they are. We will reveal their rapid advancement secrets for those interested in the climb up the corporate ladder.

We are also going to cover tactical sales maneuvers. We asked award winners throughout the country for their best secrets. Once you see them, you will be convinced they will work for you.

Before Step 1

"Until one is committed, there is hesitance, the chance to draw back, always ineffectiveness. Concerning all acts of initiative (and creation) there is an elementary truth, the ignorance of which kills countless ideas and splendid plans: That the moment one definitely commits oneself, then providence moves too. All sorts of things occur to help one that would never otherwise have occurred. A whole stream of events issues from the decision, raising in one's favor all manner of unforeseen incidents and meetings and material assistance, which no man could have dreamed would have come his way.
Whatever you can do, or dream you can; begin it!
Boldness has genius, power, and magic in it. Only engage and the mind grows heated; begin and the task will be completed."

—Johann Wolfgang von Goethe

Before you jump into Step 1, ponder two things. Two percent of those people who read this book will complete the following task first. Those 2 percent will absolutely blow away the other 98 percent in terms of effectiveness and accomplishment their whole lives.

You must have a goal. Write your goal down on a 3-by-5 card and put it in a place where you will see it every day. People who write down their goals crush those who do not. This is true in the business world and in life. Napoleon Hill said, "*A goal is a dream with a deadline.*" Thomas Carlyle is quoted as saying, "A *man without a goal is like a ship without a rudder.*" Writing down goals is critical to meeting your objectives.

Under the goal, write down two reasons why you want to obtain that goal. In this case, two reasons you want to become an incredible sales rep. This is your purpose, which adds meaning to your goal. Our purpose is not only to provide for our families but also to improve lives through contributions to medical research and worthy causes.

Finally, share this information with three people who care about you. Reread the quote by Von Goethe at the beginning of this section. By telling people what you are doing, you accomplish two *huge* things. You commit yourself to the cause and make yourself accountable. These people will also ask how you are progressing with your goals. You will want to give them positive responses.

You also indirectly elicit their help in reaching your goals. Good relationships have the power to make anything happen. Simply start the ball rolling and others will want to see you succeed and try to help you.

We cannot stress enough the power of these four paragraphs. This alone can propel some people to achieve their dreams.

Understanding Your Sales Model

"The dictionary is the only place that success comes before work. Hard work is the price we must pay for success. I think you can accomplish anything if you are willing to pay the price."
—Vince Lombardi

There are unlimited methods to gain business from your competitors in this industry. There are, however, only four cornerstone sales models from which you can belong. The models have nothing to do with specific selling strategies and tactics; rather they are overall images we portray to a customer. The models are:

- The Clinical Model
- The Partner Model
- The Friend Model
- The Cheap Model

You have actually already selected one for yourself… you just might not know it. Your customers perceive you under one of these models as we speak. Knowing the pluses and minuses of each one makes you aware of your own possible strengths and weaknesses. Great reps can even use a different model from customer to customer depending on the situation. Once you understand the four models, you gain the flexibility to choose the right model for any sales situation.

The Clinical Model

The rep using the clinical model has highly regarded clinical skills that pertain to their products and the product's relationship to patients. A rep's experience might include having worked in a hospital, working for a doctor or having some form of medical related degree. The rep using the clinical model tends to leverage their degree or clinical experience with product knowledge in order to gain business.

Everyone should aspire to the key tendencies in this model. We do that by reading and understand all the white papers and clinical documents issued on our particular products. There is a base level of clinical knowledge that nurses and physicians will **demand** that we know. Usually, that base knowledge is not enough to make you ultra successful. Early clinical related slip-ups can lose customers. Study diligently so you stay ahead. (Some top Cardiac Pacing reps study and read information for two hours per day. Not everyone will have to study this hard, but use it as a baseline for comparison.)

This clinical model is a powerful way to get and keep long-term business with customers. People like working with clinical experts. Doctors and their patients depend on our knowledge, so continual reading and learning is a must. If you have this knowledge, everyone around you will know it by the way you speak and answer questions. This knowledge is as valuable as anything we present about selling. Your clinical abilities might save a patient's life one day and earn a doctor's business for life. We have seen this happen.

The major pitfall of this model occurs when reps become dependent solely on clinical knowledge. They can grow lazy and forget to continue to sell themselves and the products they represent. Clinical people are accustomed to taking direction from a physician. Doctors are responsible for bringing in new patients and generating the income. The hospital pays them a salary to work and take care of patients. Everybody is happy. Once they transition to sales reps, this is no longer the case. Sales representatives are ultimately responsible for generating their own income.

This model, in its pure form, is our favorite model to sell against. Clinical people are used to taking care of clinical things. Their mental basis for success or failure comes from the service they provide to their patients. It is easy to lose focus on building new business, and the rep could stop exploring for new opportunities.

Clinical model reps believe (as most of us do) that the use of their product is in the best interest of their patients. When a doctor does not select their product, the pure clinical reps often tend to personalize it, leading to a defeated attitude. DO NOT LET THIS HAPPEN TO YOU or a competitive rep will come after your business!

Pure clinical model sales reps must **consciously plan** their selling activities **in advance**. Keep sales goals in front of you. It provides the focus that you need.

Key point for the rep with a clinical background: Remember what pays the bills — your selling ability. Have constant selling goals that you are reaching for. Example: I am going to meet "x" new people this week. I am going to call on Dr. "X" who has never used me before.

Key point for the rest of us: Learn as much clinical information as possible, it will help drive sales and make you more of an expert.

Remember, too: Any sales professional who is a clinical master (as it pertains to your products and specialty) and has great sales skills is vital to any company. This person has mega market value as well.

The Partner Model

Most companies emphasize this powerful model in their training. The idea behind it is to find win-win situations for your company and the hospital or doctor. This is your basic features and benefits selling. You may have heard or used one of the following lines:

"Doctor, when you use our product, your patients will receive the following benefits . . ."

Or "Mr. Purchasing Manager, if you use our product, your hospital will receive the following benefits . . ." "Does it not make sense to partner with us in light of this incredible information?"

We are taking the time to laugh at ourselves for falling into this stereotypical sales presentation. Although we have to understand the benefits of our products, Vendesi Group believes there is a better way to partner.

We prefer to use the Partner Model with doctors and hospitals in areas outside of our obvious interests. We work to add value in our customers' lives in ways that are completely unrelated to our product line. More and more high-quality companies are starting to do this. They have learned the power of this new twist on an old model.

Here is an example we have used successfully. The last time you visited a doctor as a patient, a charge sheet documented your visit. The doctor circled each diagnostic test or procedure performed on you. These procedures have codes associated with them. Doctors spend thousands of dollars each year paying someone to input these codes for Medicare, Medicaid and insurance providers. If errors are made inputting these codes, the doctors lose money. Implement the new Partner Model here.

This is how it works. The medical company arranges a meeting between the doctor's staff and a staff of reimbursement specialists – paid for by your company. The specialists "audit" the doctor's existing coding procedures. If there are mistakes being made, the specialists provide the proper coding method to eliminate expensive mistakes. This is an incredible service to physicians and directly affects their bottom line.

This is one example of our Partner Model version — providing assistance outside of normal product related services. This twist accomplishes several things. It shows the doctors that both you (because you set it up) and your company (they paid for it) are interested in supporting their business. The most important immediate benefit for you is your level of *access* in that office and to the doctors will increase.

There is another benefit as well. It is the benefit of an unspoken quid pro quo. Even though there can be no official payoff for these types of services, people tend to remember those who help them. It is human nature to want to help those who help us. Many times they remember these special services when it is time to implant a product or write a script!

There are other ways to help doctors achieve their goals. Check with your manager to see what programs your company currently offers **and what is legal and ethical** in your situation. Also, keep your eyes and ears open around your physicians. If you hear them complain about *any problem you can solve*, an opportunity for you may be close at hand.

Key point: Look for partnering opportunities in new areas as well as the common ones.

Key LEGAL point: In our example, we taught our customers bill coding as it pertained to our products and the procedures they are used on. Check with your manager or legal department on specifics for any program you want to utilize.

The Friend Model

The next two models are the most difficult to sell against. Reps use the friend model when they build friendships with customers outside of the workplace to help influence the decisions those customers make in their practices. It has often been said in business that "ties" are ultimately won by friends. Simply stated, if all else is equal the friend will win the business. This is probably true a high percentage, if not all, of the time. We would wager the friend also wins many times when everything else is not equal.

No matter how hard you try, this model cannot be used with all of your customers. You will never have enough in common with everyone to forge this kind of relationship. But, you can use it with some. There are two ways that we found to make this model work. The first way is to find customers that have common interests that you share. It helps if both of you are passionate about one of them. Some interests include:

Golf	Fishing	Football	Hunting
Biking	Skiing	Running	Children
Wine	Books	Food	History

Never attempt to use or establish the Friend Model during a first or second meeting. Build a cordial relationship first while you are discovering their outside interests. Most of these interests can be discovered easily by asking the ancillary people who work with your intended target. Bond *gradually* by talking about these common activities and interests.

Then use some savvy. Drop the doctors some information you found about your topic that might be interesting to them. If you discover an article in the newspaper or a magazine that is especially good, cut it out. Drop it by their office. Write a short note saying how you thought they might like this article. Do not write anything on your note about a product or your company. That would defeat the entire purpose. Stick to using this only occasionally and with one of your targets. After you do this once, you will get a good sense of whether it was successful with that customer. The more a customer loves a particular interest, the more effective this idea becomes.

Another strong way to formulate a friendship is to find customers that are in similar "life circumstances" as yourself. There are usually some customers in your age group. They might even have kids the same age as yours. Just these two things provide discussion points you can both relate to. You might even attend the same church, eat at the same restaurants or watch the same movies and TV shows. Actively listen for the outside interests of your target customers. This activity is time well spent in building your territory as *your* practice.

Some people are naturally good at this and some are not. Whatever category you are in, consciously work on building your friendships. Everyone should keep a list (mental or physical) of all customers' outside interests. If you build your list and review it regularly, approaching your customers becomes easy.

Key point: The friendship model is potentially the most powerful of all models.

The Cheap Model

This is the final selling model and one that we hate to compete against. It works exactly as it sounds. The cheap model sales rep <u>always</u> has the least expensive product in town. If you are selling under this model with your entire line of products, you might be in trouble. As a matter of fact, you are in trouble. Start looking for a new company to work for. The reason for this is simple. If a company is always trying to be a low-cost leader (even if they are not trying to, but are anyway), you as the sales rep become the most expensive part of their equation. Sooner or later downsizing will eliminate your position, or your territory geography will become huge. A friend of ours found himself at one of these companies. Now his territory is the whole country!

Never use the cheap model. In fact, you want to be selling the most expensive products in the hospital or doctor's office. You want to be a financial burden to the hospital. This might sound controversial, but it is true. If you are a financial burden to the hospital, that generally means your products are **vital**. That is position A. Vital products bring big profits and big commissions.

It has been said repeatedly in sales that if you win on price, you will ultimately lose on price. Endeavor to be better as a professional medical sales rep. Look for and convey all the reasons your products should demand a price premium. Then keep the price up.

It is okay to have some products in your bag that are low-cost, generic items. But, you absolutely must have those high ticket items in your bag as well.

"Companies price their products for exactly what they think they are worth." – **Ryan Gray**

A Game Plan or Base Sales Strategy

"Strategy without tactics is the slowest route to victory.
Tactics without strategy is the noise before defeat."
—Sun Tzu

Regardless of which model you use, you need some selling method or system to guide you. The ultimate purpose of this book is not to teach a specific selling system for your business. There are plenty of these books already on the market. Our group has participated in many advanced sales training courses that teach selling systems. Some of them include the following:

The Harvard Negotiation Project
The Richardson Co. Consultative Selling
Stop Telling, Start Selling
SPIN Selling
ACE Sales Training
Sandler Sales Training

These advanced sales training courses represent just those companies we tracked. The only system we think is worth your time is David Sandler's advanced sales training system. David Sandler, in our opinion, should be deemed as the father of all selling systems. Mr. Sandler passed away in 1995, but his expertise in selling continues to prove to be the best. Devour anything and everything on his methods.

His materials cover:

- Up front contracting
- Finding a prospect's pain – everyone buys to ease pain
- All matters concerning money
- Leading people to a decision
- Post selling procedures

Then the stuff we really like:

- When and how to play dumb. Everyone should know how and when to "not know" an answer.
- Reverse Negative Selling (absolute best single weapon in sales)
- How to STOP selling features and benefits

Though there are plenty of books that give great sales tips, throw away every book that teaches a specific sales method. Once you have seen the Sandler system work, you will understand why we give the advice. The others are a waste of your time and shelf space.

"You Cannot Teach a Kid to Ride a Bike at a Seminar" is Sandler's best-known title and is available at vendesigroup. com. Listen to Sandler tapes as you drive around your territory as well. There might even be a Sandler group (called the President's Club) that meets in your area.

It is vital for you as a representative in the medical field to pick a selling system. According to Sandler, "If you do not have a selling system of your own when you are face to face with a prospect; you will unknowingly default to the prospect's system." You must be in control of the process and guide your prospects to your desired conclusion. If you have no sequential steps to move customers through the selling cycle, they will not become your customers.

The Sandler system is the only one we endorse because we personally know it works! Using the system will set you above your competitors and other sales reps within your company. If you look over the Sandler system and just do not think it is right for you, get some system that works for you and perfect it. Do not let prospects run your sales calls.

Open Access

"Access is earned, given or taken."
—Ryan Gray

Open Access is critical in this business. Having open access is defined simply as your ability to move around in doctor's offices, operating rooms, lounges or wherever your doctors and customers work without being asked to leave.

Several key factors affect your level of access:

- How long your customers have known you
- The quality of their relationship with you
- Your proven ability to be helpful in different situations

One of our top priorities in the field was building access to the point of walking into any hospital in our territories, then straight into the operating room. No one ever asked us a question.

That is the ultimate access you want to build.

Access also means that you do not have to make an appointment.

Top-notch salespeople rarely need appointments to conduct their business. Test this the next time you would normally make an appointment. Tell your customer you will be by on a given day. Do not be more specific than that. The customer's response will indicate your level of access. If this customer demands a time to meet, your access (and relationship) is not very high. Work to improve it.

Here are a few things to remember about access.

- **Every interaction** you have can potentially build your access level.

- Follow hospital protocol every time. Do not barge into an operating room solely to check your access. It must be built slowly. **Never risk being banned from a hospital.**

- Some reps believe that customers must like us in order to be granted this access. That is an incorrect assumption. You only need the hospital or the physician to **not care** if you are around. This is a much easier threshold to meet. Don't pester people, and they generally won't care what you are doing.

- The more access you have, the less the "rules" will apply to you.

There are no shortcuts to building access. The real keys are:

- Being clinically helpful when consulted
- Being courteous and attentive to ancillary people surrounding your customers
- Asking a few sincere questions about people's outside lives
- Remembering those personal details for the next encounter with that person
- Following up immediately when you make a promise
- Do not loiter. Do your business and move on.

A sales call for the sole purpose of building access through one of these methods is time well spent. You are both gaining relationships and increasing your ultimate value to your company. There is a more subtle gain for you as well; here it is.

The stronger your relationships are with your customers, the higher your personal market value becomes.

Filters

Who is the doctor's information gatekeeper? Who *literally* filters out our information before it reaches the intended target? The ability to effectively and smoothly work around your customer's filters is a learned behavior. Your success depends on your personal abilities to build relationships with these people and then "eliminate" them from the process.

To overcome them you must do the following:

1. Recognize the filter. Until you know differently, **consider everyone a filter**.
2. Do not trust anyone to pass on information to your customer.
3. Sidestep the filter. Once you identify point one and enact point two, you can actively concentrate on number three.
4. In the end, know that **you** are the one who must disseminate your

information and that of your company.

The following is a prime example of a filter. A doctor requested some information on a new surgical technique from a partner in our group. The information was promptly faxed to his office. A friend in the office called a few minutes later saying she found the fax in the trash can and asked if it was important.

Several valuable lessons are learned from this example:

- If possible, **AVOID FAXING ANYTHING.**
- When a customer asks for information, use that request to create a face to face with that customer.
- Do not assume ANYTHING — even vital information — will be passed on to your customer.

Make Your Clothes Work

"Clothes make the man. Naked people have little or no influence on society."
—Mark Twain

Professional dress has been the rule of our profession regardless of your sex. Appropriate dress *could* include suits, scrubs, or some form of business casual. Some companies require you to wear a suit at all times. Most companies, however, will allow you to make dress choices for yourself.

Some sales training services will suggest you always dress up for any customer. Simply put, this means wear your best suit, best tie and flashy jewelry. They want you to appear highly successful as a sales representative. The traditional wisdom says if you wear a Rolex, you must be successful.

We do not believe this is *always* the best choice. For example, it might not be the best idea to wear a $15,000 watch to make a sales call on a customer who makes $30,000 a year. The main reason this does not make sense is you are building a long-term relationship with your customers. Trying to impress someone with fancy clothes and jewelry usually does not work over time.

Here is a perfect example. There is a retired pacing rep we know who made about $2,000,000 a year for over 20 years. He drove the same beat up truck for nearly 20 years. He never wanted his customers to think he did not need their business.

While he drove his old truck to work, his wife always drove a brand-new Jaguar. Most of his customers never knew it. This separation of business and personal life was a shrewd and smart decision.

Some people in this industry wear scrubs to 99 percent of their business dealings. This might be a good choice for several reasons. First, you drop dry cleaning as an expense in your life. Also, if you are dealing with nurses, doctors and staff at a hospital, you look just like them. Dressing like them is a form of mirroring — a good thing. Though scrubs are fine for some situations, it cannot be your only choice.

We believe varied dress is best. Our advice is you dress just a shade better than your customer. ***Your clothes should not be an issue.***

If you are pitching a product, consider your clothes as part of your presentation. Here are some guidelines for <u>sales presentations</u> but not necessarily routine maintenance of a hospital or account.

- A doctor's office – Men — at least a tie; probably a suit

   Women — a suit in most instances

   (Both — There might be patients around; so you want to inspire their confidence in the doctor by looking your best.)
- A department manager — probably a suit, but you can mirror
- A purchasing manager — dress a shade better
- A nurse manager — dress a shade better or mirror

Consider the following example of how clothes can become an issue. A sales rep worked cases in the Cath

Lab once or twice a week. He always wore scrubs. After each case, he collected a purchase order number from the materials manager who always wore a tie. The materials manager thought it was disrespectful the rep never made an effort to wear anything other than scrubs. Right or wrong, the rep was offending the materials manager's dress code.

He could have avoided the situation by wearing a tie once a month! The rep was oblivious to it and ended up losing business in the account. He never knew what hit him. ***Ensure that your clothes match the given situation at least 95 percent of the time.***

We should also note that being different could be an advantage. If every rep you compete against is wearing a suit, you might have to change something in order to stand out. Pharmaceutical reps tend to wear suits every day and everyone can see them coming. Check with your manager about wearing scrubs. Doing so might differentiate you and give you the edge in certain situations or make you seem more clinical. It might allow customers to let down their guard a bit as well.

What not to wear

In a perfect world you should be able to wear whatever reasonable clothes you like. There should be no inferences put on you because of the clothes you wear. Unfortunately, the world is not perfect. Hospitals, and people who work there, are but a microcosm of our society. They will comment on a rep's hair, clothes, accent or anything else they come up with. Many hospital employees spend all day in front of a computer screen, and we provide much needed comic relief.

Norman Vincent Peale wrote, *"It is a fact that you project what you are."*

Ultimately men and women must decide what image to portray. If ladies wear skintight skirts and low-cut blouses, you will generate perceptions about you that may not be right. Men, if you wear tight scrubs with the sleeves rolled up to show your muscles, perceptions about you will float around. In fact, some customers we know nicknamed a competitor "Buffy" because he dressed as though he were in the gym! He will <u>forever</u> carry that stigma with those customers.

No matter how beautiful or handsome you are, if you wear conservative suits and business attire you will be perceived as professional. This is the right road to travel in almost all situations.

All of these suggestions are highly dependent upon your individual style, the image you want to portray, the weather climate in which you live and a host of other factors. The guidelines are only suggestions to prevent your clothes from becoming an issue that gets between you and your success.

Anyone can bond!

Just as some men find common interests among other men (in this case their male customers), women should not be discouraged from seeking out common interests as well. Traditionally, women have allowed male reps to have the edge when "bonding" with customers around traditional male activities like sports or hunting. The lack of these commonalities made it more of a challenge to form personal relationships with some male customers.

Women really have only two options to overcome this self-perceived disadvantage. One is take an active interest in learning about the activities around which men bond. There are no laws keeping you from any outside activities that might assist you in creating personal relationships. Traditional norms as they relate to "male activities" are being brought down daily. More and more women are learning to golf primarily for the business advantages it brings. If you decide to take this route, get professional help to become as proficient as possible at the activity. Your competence will allow you to bond more effectively.

The second option was utilized very successfully by one of the members of Vendesi Group. While at Merck, she found it difficult to form good relationships with some male doctors because she did not golf, hunt or fish. She circumvented normal procedures for the back door approach and did an incredibly smart thing. She formed a great relationship with the female staff members of her best doctors (she built her access.) She then used those friendships to get to know the doctors' wives. Talk about leverage! The wives loved her and their husbands knew it.

Unfortunately, with certain new federal codes of business, *writing off* entertainment for doctors' spouses might be illegal depending on your employer. Check with your manager on the details. You can still do it on your own dime *if you have a relationship outside of work*, or the doctor can pay for his wife's meal. The law cannot keep you from meeting your friends, whoever they might be. The bottom line is we should all be looking for every available inroad to build key relationships with those difficult doctors. ***Be creative!***

Proper Targeting

"Properly selecting targets saves time and maximizes your sales potential."

—Ryan Gray

What follows is Vendesi Group's proven method of selecting, then processing sales targets.

Categorize customers by size. Categorize each customer by size. Use labels *A*, *B*, and *C* to categorize by size to differentiate them for targeting purposes. *A* and *B* accounts should make up 80 percent of your sales *potential*. *A* accounts are the largest customers you have in your territory. They represent the largest amount of potential business but may also have access barriers or layers of politics to overcome. Use sales potential as the only measuring factor for this category. Your company should be able to provide the sales potential for each of your accounts. Ask for help if this number is not provided.

Here is a trick if you are having problems putting customers into three groups. Create a list of all your accounts and their annual sales potential. As you go down the list there should be natural breaks between the huge volume users, the midrange volume users and the small volume users. Those breaks will determine the category for each account.

Know your customers. A good sales rep knows **where** the current business is — **who** the customers are, the **volume** of their business, and **why** those customers have chosen to do business with their company. The "why" is simply the hot button issue that appeals to your customers and make them select you as their supplier.

Remembering why your customers buy from you enables you to **protect that business**. Protect it by occasionally providing information that reminds the customers of those issues that made them your customers in the first place. For example, if they buy from you because of the clinical superiority of your products, drop by to deliver new clinical papers that are of interest. Tailor information individually to each customer.

Visit regularly. Visit current customers often and examine them thoroughly to determine if you are maximizing their potential. It is usually faster to grow existing business, if the opportunity exists, than to create brand new customers. If you do not know an accounts' total sales-to-potential ratio, you must find out this information quickly. Put these accounts at the top of your 30-day target list (more on the 30-day list in a moment).

Note: The total sales-to-potential ratio should be one to one. If an account has the potential to do 100 cases per month and they are doing 100 cases with you, your ratio is one to one, or 100 percent. If you are doing 90 cases, you are somehow losing 10 cases per month. There might be a variety of reasons you do not have a one-to-one ratio with a customer. Our point here is you should know the reason. There might be some easy business to pick up by answering this question.

Your target list. We support the idea of a 30-60-90 day target list. It is a simple and powerful tool to organize movement through the sales cycle with your accounts. The general premise is to receive a yes or no answer to your current proposal in 30 days for those customers on your 30-day list. One way or the other, they should be off the list in the next 30 days and replaced with new opportunities. The same principle is applied to 60 and 90-day targets. Using this tool allows you to track movement of your sales processes to their ultimate conclusions. If used correctly, accounts/customers will continually move from 90 to 60 to 30 — then off the list and are replaced.

In general, most medical sales are not same day sales and have medium to long sales cycles. Regardless of the length of your sales cycle, your target list will still be full. Targets can either be complete hospitals or individual decision makers that are a piece of the larger picture. If you have an empty target list, you are saying there is no expectation of closing any new business in the current quarter or receiving a yes or no answer from a decision maker. If your target list is empty, we believe you are not asking for anything from your customers. When sales people fail to ask for new business, agreements or opportunities, their sales will stagnate every time. **Always be asking for something.**

Accounts and customers can move fluidly back and forth on your target list, but try to move them sequentially from 90 to 60 to 30 to off. Sometimes outside influences cause a target to move the other direction, but make this a rare occurrence. Remember that a customer who actually commits to a "no" is a good thing. "No" is better than "maybe". "No" allows us to move on and not waste time. A "maybe" can linger forever and is probably just a "no."

"'Maybe' is the ultimate killer of the effective use of time."

—Ryan Gray

Start targeting. After you categorize your accounts you are ready to start targeting. Consider current customers with untapped potential, accounts with quick selling cycles (few decision makers) and everything else you know about targeting.

The *B* accounts are usually the best choices for your 30-60-90 day plan. Those accounts make up significant sales potential with minimal time to conversion. At least in theory these accounts should convert easier than larger accounts due to their smaller number of decision makers and possible smaller bureaucracy. It is certainly possible to have a moderate-sized account that is a huge headache to convert or a huge one that flips in a day. This is where specific information is needed to fine-tune your plan.

It is always good to have at least one *A* account on your target list. You might have to break out an *A* account into individual decision makers. By this I mean, if several people are involved, list them separately. Overall, continue to pursue the accounts that can move the largest amount of revenue in the shortest amount of time.

Customer's geographic location. If you are deciding between two similar accounts for your target list, geographical advantage breaks a tie. Those accounts close to your home base or close to your competitor's home base should receive higher priority.

Know where your competitive reps live. They **will** spend more time calling on accounts in their hometowns. You might have to spend more time in these areas to compensate.

Your target list is your *strategic* sales plan for the current quarter. It is the big picture of what you are trying to accomplish. We will add multiple, *tactical* selling strategies in the remainder of this book.

As a final note: Most reps should spend the majority of their time in front of non-customers. This is by far the best way to grow your dollar revenue. If you find yourself spending your sales time with current customers and friends, you can only grow your business at the same rate they grow their business.

All About Selling to Doctors

"Is it not also true that no physician, in so far as he is a physician, considers or enjoins what is for the physician's interest, but that all seek the good of their patients? For we have agreed that a physician strictly so called, is a ruler of bodies, and not a maker of money, have we not?"
—Plato, Greek Philosopher BC 427-347

Plato is not alive today!

In order to succeed in this business, you must be comfortable selling to doctors. That comfort comes with time and practice. Egos run rampant with both doctors <u>and</u> high-powered, highly paid salespeople. (As a matter of fact, the *average* doctor probably does not earn much more money than a well-compensated medical rep.) While 99 percent of medical salespeople are stroking doctors' egos, be the 1 percent that does not.

The difference between them and you is that doctors chose to go to medical school. They have years of training in medical practice so they are naturally going to know more about practicing medicine than we do. It does not mean they are better people than we – though it often seems they believe that!

Do not be intimidated by their status. Be respectful and courteous but stay assured that you bring value to the table. The more value you add, the more you will be respected for your contribution and your confidence.

To make sales to doctors, you must have the ability to physically get yourself in front of doctors. There are many methods that are used successfully and unsuccessfully. In fact, one rep might try something on a doctor and have no success. Another rep walks in right after, making the same pitch and walks away with the sale. We will cover some of these tactics later.

Our goal is to help you avoid spending countless hours in a doctor's waiting room reading last year's issue of "*US Magazine*". What an incredible waste of time! (At least bring the latest journal or white paper to review if you are absolutely stuck.)

From a Doctor's Perspective

Now that we spent some time considering you and your style, let us consider how doctors think in regard to their interaction with us. Doctors have essentially two ways of choosing the medical companies with whom they associate. The first choice is to partner solely with one company. The second is to play the field. Both have pluses and minuses. Let us outline the ins and outs of each to add to your insight while planning and interacting.

The doctor who works solely with one company

You need a few of these doctors in your account portfolio. They tend to be loyal and will use you over and over again. They try your new things first and are slow to try a competitor. These are the best customers you can have.

From the doctors' point of view, going with an individual company for all needs in a particular area ensures they get first crack at any new products the company brings to the market. If they choose a stagnant company (or a company with consistently low market share or little research and development money), they might (and should in our opinion) get left out for a while when new products arrive in the market.

Swaying doctors from a competitor to your side under this scenario can be tricky; doing so usually takes a bit of time. There are several things you can try to speed up the process. Here are a few good ones:

1. Invite them to a plant tour or an educational meeting in a nice place. It is great to get them out of town and begin building a relationship away from normal business.

2. Invite them to dinner with a vice president (or higher) within your organization. Many upper level managers are happy to help you with important customers. Always go through your manager, but "demand" that a high value manager/officer come to dinner.

3. Gently point out to the doctors the risks of partnering with only one company. They are but one recall away from serious problems for them and their patients. (Of course, your competitors should be pointing this out to all your loyal customers. Again, be gentle.)

4. Use our partnering model and look for ways you can help grow their business.

The doctor who plays the field

There are doctors who make a conscious effort to utilize several or all the companies that supply products to their specialty. From their standpoint, they receive better service from all their reps (because they know all the companies are vying for their business) and will receive new products that arrive on the market from everyone.

By playing the field, the doctors are saying there is no *significant* clinical difference in the products in their minds. There may be other reasons as well, but we will assume the products are similar.

Ancillary staff can play a key role in winning these customers. Build a relationship with anyone who works with this type of doctor. Be over-the-top with your customer service for these people.

Here are some more considerations when you target this type of doctor:

- Spend extra time treating their staff well, and it can pay off for you.
  - o Offer continuing education credits
  - o Invite them to happy hours
  - o Bring them food
- Instead of trying to win all the business at once, try to get pieces.
- Never accept just a share of the business over the long term.
- Be subtly aggressive while going after more business in the ways we outline in this book.

Some Tactical Tips

Know where the doctor is on every day of the week

Doctors are creatures of habit. They generally do the exact same thing on one Monday as they do the following Monday. They do the same thing on one Tuesday as they do the following Tuesday.

Know their complete schedules. Except for a few variances, most doctors will consistently work on a very similar schedule. Use this knowledge to your advantage.

Vendesi Group designed a simple but effective software program called DoctorTrak™©. The program allows you to click any day and instantly see where your doctors will be (office, lab, OR, etc.) and what time they will be there on that day! Regardless of your system, you *must know* exactly where all your doctors are every hour.

DoctorTrak™© is inexpensive and simply too good a tool not to have! Our entire group utilizes this software. A free 30-day trial is available for download at www.vendesigroup.com.

Key selling points and marketing messages

When you have a key selling point to discuss with your doctors (or customers), there is one way to make certain they receive it. Use a spreadsheet and write down the key point, as the title, at the top of the page. Then, list every customer that needs to hear the message. Leave room for a target date and a remarks section. Then simply work down the list and cross off names as you go. This simple and effective method will guarantee that your messages get out.

Many companies now mandate this process or one like it. Millions of dollars are spent every year in the marketing department of your company. Those dollars are ultimately wasted if their messages are not delivered. Remember, the marketing department's sole reason for existence is increasing your sales revenue. Never let their work go to waste.

Keeping track of your selling points and your doctors' locations will make your life easy for any number of reasons. A main benefit is that you can plan your week. Just doing these two things will separate you from 95 percent of all other medical sales reps who are flying by the seat of their pants. Check your doctor location against your Key Selling Point list, and you are ready to go. You are organized with specific messages to deliver to specific doctors. A more detailed discussion of marketing messages is coming.

Getting clinical information to your doctors

If your company provides you with a new clinical paper that favorably regards your product, do the following:

- Take it to a copy store and make a copy for each of your doctors (or order copies, depending on the copyright law).
- Write their names on them or include an individualized cover page for each customer.
- Then pass them out.

By doing this with useful papers (or any other critical material), you guarantee that all your doctors get the information. This is a powerful tip, similar to the previous one but specific to clinical papers.

Clinical application meetings, plant tours and new-product training

Offsite clinical application, training meetings or plant tours are an essential part of product sales. These sessions generally allow you and your doctor/customer to fly to fun locations for advanced training. A wide range of topics may include technical training on the use of your products, new product technology, market trends, new applications of old procedures and government regulations.

Take advantage of every such opportunity provided by your company. There is no better way to build a relationship with your doctors than to spend three days away from work with them. Consequently, companies spend millions of dollars a year on these programs. **They spend the money because the programs work.**

Here is a trick to make sure your customers will always be invited to these meetings. **Track each of your attending customer's purchases both before and after each meeting.** Ninety-nine percent of the reps in your company do not do this (the company might, but most reps do not).

- Track this number for each customer who goes to the meeting.
- When the next meeting is scheduled, show your manager and the marketing team your customer track record.
- Show them your understanding of the process and your ability to choose good targets that get positive results.
- Show a positive dollar impact for the company.

It will be an easy choice for your company to invite your target customers if you follow this process.

Here are some other good points. Since you will probably arrange the flight reservations for the meeting, attempt to fly with your customer. You can utilize the flying time to further your personal relationship. Do not talk about products, but use the time to bond. If you start in different cities, arrange the connecting flights in the same city so you can fly the final leg together. Even better, if feasible, fly or drive to your customer's initial leg and take the whole trip together.

Clinical trials

Companies use clinical trials, clinical surveys and other methods to make clinical evaluations of their products. Properly used, these tools are very powerful in gaining new business. For example, if a doctor's current reimbursement is $1200 for a colonoscopy and you give him/her $600 to try your product and provide feedback after the case, you have just increased their revenue for the case by 50 percent.

These programs provide a great opportunity to sell your products if the doctor is not currently using you or to say thank you to a loyal customer. This business practice is becoming widely used in our profession.

Use these tools as often as possible. If your company does not participate in these programs, try to find out why. Then, campaign to get some started. Just follow FDA protocol in gathering data and you will stay out of trouble.

Next, you must carefully decide whom to target for these trials. Doing this may prove to be a little trickier than you might first assume. Take the following things into consideration:

1. Who your current customers are
2. Who your current targets are
3. Where can you easily reach geographically?
4. Your ability to gain access to the doctors and hospitals
5. Can a hospital manage the paperwork load of a clinical trial?
6. Where can you realize an acceptable revenue gain?

These are but a few considerations you face. Do you want to use the trial to go after new business? Do you want to use the trial to reward loyal customers? Unfortunately, there is no right answer that will work every time. Have serious conversations with your manager about which customers get your clinicals. The most obvious choice is not always the correct choice.

The primary reason anyone performs a clinical trial or survey is to generate new business. Maximizing the return of a clinical trial or survey is critical to the success of your company. Research and development money is valuable to your company and to your customer. Use this money wisely, and you will stay on the top of the marketing department's list for future trials.

Also pay attention to:

The doctor's hospital. Is the hospital able to handle the paperwork and strict guidelines that accompany a clinical trial (certainly consider this if you are participating in an FDA pre-market trial)? Do you have good access to the account? In other words, can you contend with the gatekeeper standing in your way at every turn? Does the hospital have a history of prompt payments for clinical trial products?

Other doctors who work in that hospital. Will doctors work together to complete your trial? If all doctors are not included, do you risk losing those doctors' business because they are not involved?

Competitive politics between doctors. Doctors are competitive. Even doctors within the same group will compete for referrals, patients and publishing opportunities. Some doctors will not participate unless they are listed as a principal investigator. Even the order that doctors' names appear on the published work is negotiated. Consider how this plays out.

The hospitals and doctors who are not in your trial. If your trial is large enough, all doctors in town will know about it. They will also know which doctors were selected by your company to perform the trial. If the doctors who are not included in the trial are good customers, there is a better than average possibility you will lose their business. This loss may or may not be short term. Doctors love to show us (as reps and companies) who the ultimate boss is.

These are only some of the keys to focus on. Try to look at clinical trials from every possible angle. Then make the best selection. There is always the distinct possibility of damaging some of your business or of hurting a relationship when doling out trials. Make sure your gain is much higher than your loss.

Consider a smaller, but busy, out-of-town hospital for your trial. The political fallout will most likely be minimal. If it is high on your list of targets, it will be a big win with small downside consequences. The fewer people who know about your trial initially, the better off you may be. Again, the entire purpose of trials is to increase product sales either with new products or existing ones. If you have ground breaking new products, everyone will hear about them in due time.

Your Clinical Opinions

"Science is the father of knowledge, but opinion breeds ignorance."

—Hippocrates

The more clinically adept you become with your products, the more you may generate personal opinions about a patient's ultimate treatment when selling and interacting with doctors. In other words, you may become so supportive of your products and services that you believe doctors are in borderline malpractice if they do not follow your recommendations. We have seen this scenario acted out countless times. The ultimate conclusion is always the same. Reps who could not control their emotions lost the doctor's business — usually forever. We have also seen a rep get fired for this.

A positive attitude toward your products is great to have. You ***should*** believe in yourself, your company and your product. However, ***never*** imply that a doctor is making a wrong decision by choosing one of your competitor's devices. Often a rep feels so strongly about a product that the rep gets angry if a doctor chooses a different course of action. To protect the relationship, use your selling skills. Share your thoughts but respectfully allow doctors to form their own conclusions. Accept the fact that not every doctor will agree with every argument you make.

Point two. As your clinical knowledge continues to grow, your experiences will ultimately lead you to judgments as to whether a doctor is either a good purveyor of medicine or a poor one. You will certainly have your opinions of who the best doctors are within your specialty.

Never comment on the skills, or lack thereof, of any physician to anyone. Even if that doctor's performance is the worst you have ever seen, and you would not let them touch the neighbor's dog that barks all night! You must remain silent!

Doing otherwise will always come back to haunt you. Just be happy that they use your products and continue to give them your best service.

A doctor we work with was overheard making the following comment when asked why he used a particular rep. He said, "I use him (the rep) because he keeps his damn mouth shut." There are ears in every nook and cranny of a hospital or doctor's office. Gossip will spread in these places as easily as anywhere else. Do not be a part of it.

Medicine is a trade off. Patients receive a benefit at the cost of something else. One drug might help with kidney disease while at the same time causing dizziness and fatigue. Or, patients must tolerate some form of pain (i.e. surgery) in order to ultimately feel better. These trade offs occur in every facet of the patient's treatment phase and with every product a doctor chooses.

All the products we sell have trade offs. Doctors ultimately bear the stress of making these tough decisions and dealing with the aftermath. As sales reps, our job is to present the case for our products to the best of our abilities and then allow our customers to make a choice. The more persuasive we are with our arguments, the more sales we will make over our working lifetimes.

Selling to Nurses

Many of our partners began their careers selling primarily to nurses. Then gradually, doctors took over as our primary customers. Looking back, we would do things differently as it pertains to our approach to nurses. We would treat nurses more like doctors.

Specifically, we would find key decision makers, give them the dog and pony show and invite them to lunch and dinner. In short, we would have built relationships with them as we now do with doctors. Nurses are generally more loyal than their doctor colleagues! A good one will also stand up for you in your absence.

There is something that we would stop doing as well. We would stop buying breakfast and lunch for groups of nurses who are not key decision makers. This is a poor use of your time and a worse use of your budget as many of these people are not even influencers. Do what you must but be conscious of where your money is going.

If nurses are your decision makers, treat them like doctors.

Selling to purchasing agents

Purchasing agents are usually support staff, though there are unique times where they play a role in clinical decision-making. Our philosophy is to gather information from them and give little or nothing back. In fact, we want to work the hospital without their department even knowing what we are doing.

Always follow hospital protocol, but we believe it is better to inform purchasing when the job is done than to warn them about your upcoming sales efforts. The reason there is some friction between them and us is twofold. First, we spend their money! Second, our sales successes create work for them — updating computers with new codes, signing purchasing contracts, signing inventory agreements and creating par levels, etc. A single product change in a hospital can require a 100-step process to be initiated to accommodate the changes.

The more time that you spend in the purchasing departments, the more rules and red tape you will encounter. It is easier to ask for forgiveness than get permission in most cases.

Create $1,000,000 in Sales with One Idea? You bet…and Here are 23!

"In the valley of the blind, the one-eyed man is king."
—Gerard Didier Erasmus

One million dollars in sales from one idea? You better believe it! Each of the following information-packed mini-sections provides you with a concept that can make or break a sales relationship at a critical time. Consciously thinking about them can easily add that $1 million in sales to your territory — often in only 12 months.

If you have difficulty in believing this and prefer the long-term approach, look at it this way. An average-sized territory can range from $2,000,000 to $10,000,000 per year. Let us take something in the middle like $5,000,000. Over a 25-year career, that is $125,000,000 that passes through your hands. One hundred and twenty five million dollars! It is easy to calculate that these ideas, representing over 100 years of medical sales experience, can gross you an extra million. Actually, they should make you an extra 10 to 35 million dollars! We prefer to think BIG; 12 months is all you need.

There is also a single key personality trait that supercharges these ideas. In fact, all good managers should carefully determine a candidate's level of this trait before a hiring decision is made. That trait is a ***sense of urgency***. It can be learned, but it takes a great deal of work or an extreme situation.

Of necessity, your author developed this trait quickly while selling in the Cardiac Rhythm Management (pacing and defibrillation) field. In that field – on a daily basis — a rep can receive up to 30 pages of critical action items from customers. Each customer who sends those pages expects to be satisfied today! Urgency is learned very quickly.

Individuals displaying this particular trait are usually excellent sales reps. Develop it in yourself by taking immediate action on *to do* items that come up for your customers.

Do not procrastinate on anything; to do items build up quickly.

It became apparent while writing this book that most people do not share our sense of urgency. Many editors, publishers, web designers or software writers we worked with respond at their own pace, not that of their customers.

They might not know, but it costs them money. They also might not care. In the medical field there is a limited customer base for our products and a rep cannot afford to be unresponsive. Constantly work to be faster and more efficient in meeting customer requests and these ideas will work even better.

Now the $1,000,000 ideas.

#1 It is easier to keep existing customers than it is to find new ones

Always pay attention to your current users and keep them happy. Visit every customer, regardless how small, on a routine basis. Each customer deserves your attention. Take customers for granted and you risk losing their business to another company that placed a higher value on their business. It is very difficult to regain an account you lose due to your inattention!

Even if the account is small, check in on them once a year to see if anything has changed. You might even find a new opportunity where one never existed before.

#2 Out of sight, out of mind

The medical marketplace is overflowing with competitors. Many times, the rep who is in the hospital when a product is needed receives the implant, the referral or the script. Be there! There is a pacemaker rep we know who is fairly inept at most things he does. But, he is always in his accounts. Even if he is reading the newspaper in the doctor's lounge or drinking coffee in a lab, he maximizes his visibility at all times. He gives the perception that he is there, ready to help, and his doctors know it. He gets ALL his business this way (earning well over $200,000 per year). If this concept did not work, reps would not book entire days in labs. Companies understand if their reps are in the department, they get the sale and the commission.

#3 The medical sales law of unintended consequences

By being in your marketplace physically, good things happen. Eat in the cafeteria at your hospitals or grab snacks at their machines. Take your time there and run into people. Most doctors round in the morning from 6:30 until their cases begin or they have office clinic. (Where they round will depend on their specialty.)

Grab a cup of coffee and the paper and "just happen to be" between the ICU and the OR, lab or office. Many times a wave is all you get. But think of yourself as a billboard for your company. You just received a drive-by hit! **Be careful using this technique. It will usually work but can go south if it is overused.**

Nearly every time you make a physical call in an office or hospital, you get what we call a "Bump into." A "Bump into" occurs when you are on your way to a meeting or case and "Bump into" a customer in a hallway, a lounge, a restroom, the parking lot or anyplace else. These unintended face-to-face meetings are the bonuses for just being at work. Do not force or fake these "Bump into" meetings.

We have heard stories about reps cornering doctors in parking lots. You might as well pack your bags and find a new business if you are one of these bottom-dwellers. A "Bump into" is accidental by nature. So just be happy with the contact. Say "Hello," or comment on a mutual interest if they have a second and move on.

Strike up real conversations only if you have an excellent relationship with the customers or if they are willing to talk. Do not use these opportunities to talk business. The purpose is only to build a relationship.

If you cannot talk to a doctor about anything other than business, you will never be seen as anything more than a sales rep.

#4 Lessons about the ICU

Know the power of the ICU or hospital floors. **Be careful in the use of this technique; some reps should not try it!** Read on to see why.

These areas have long been a sanctuary for doctors. But, if you have a medical job that requires patient interaction in these areas, you hold a great advantage over reps who do not. The ICU/hospital-unit barrier that exists for the rest of the medical sales community does not exist for you. Your job forces you to spend time in the ICU doing post op follow up on patients, etc. Nurses and doctors are not opposed to your being there or to discussing patient issues with you at this time.

If you are a clever sales rep, you **can and should** use this time to promote specific advantages that your products are providing to the patients. I say "clever" because you want to talk up your product advantages without overtly talking them up. Use specific advantages of your products as they relate to a specific patient in the hospital. If you understand this, you will have success. If you do not, you will likely not be welcome here for anything other than your immediate job.

It is possible to meet a doctor in the ICU if you do not have an appointment. Here is the catch and it is a big one. You better have a darn good reason (information about a specific patient for example) or an excellent relationship to meet with customers there. It **cannot** be typical day-to-day selling, or again, you will be asked to leave and could get thrown out of the hospital. If it is urgent, important to your customer or an emergency, you can use the ICU or hospital floors.

Use the ICU to your advantage if you can, but if you don't have a legitimate purpose there, we have plenty of million-dollar ideas you can use.

#5 Face to face's

Getting in front of doctors and key decision makers is difficult. Use every opportunity to create face-to-face time with them. **Never** call, leave messages at the office, e-mail or voice mail your key customers — if a face to face can be accomplished. If you have information to share you think is important, then it is important enough to deliver by hand. Just getting in front of doctors from week to week, month to month and year after year is tough. You have to be creative and look for any and every excuse you can to create face-to-face meetings with your customers.

The following is a small list of items that should be communicated face to face.

- Invitations to dinner

- New clinical white papers that make a difference in their practice
- Articles you find about their "fun button" issues — golf, wine, travel, etc.
- Information pertaining to a specific patient of theirs
- Notification that your company provided gratis products to the hospital

If you give a product to a hospital for an indigent patient, consider giving every physician you work with at that hospital a letter describing your donation. The ultimate purpose is to advertise your good will.

If your job allows you frequent face-to-face contacts with your customers, remember this: Do not take these contacts for granted. Remember again that you are a walking billboard for your company and yourself (as well as your commission check!) Every time customers see you, a subconscious thought about you is recorded.

Even if you are together often, continue to communicate as much as possible in person. Communicating this way also maximizes your "Bump into's" with other customers which can be very valuable for your business and the way you are perceived. No one ever received a free "Bump into" while sending a fax or calling on the phone. It just keeps you fresh on the minds of your customers. You will earn extra business this way.

#6 Join or start a journal club

Many university settings (and other hospitals as well) host journal clubs. These are usually monthly meetings where doctors discuss the pertinent articles published in their trade journals. Sometimes these meetings are open and other times they are not. Ask ALL of your doctors if they participate in these clubs. If they do, simply make a note of it for later use. Do NOT immediately ask anything else. Bring up your questions at a later date.

You might not be able to attend, but there are other things you can do. Bring by interesting articles to each participating doctor as possible journal-club material. They might discuss your article among their group. If you do this, make SURE the article cannot be picked apart. In other words, do not give them anything unless you know for certain there is nothing damning about your product stated. Some of these are very intense and scientific! Know and understand every word before you give it out. You might get questioned on it as well. Attend the meeting if possible.

If you cannot find an established journal club, consider starting one yourself. Your attendance will be best if your meeting is scheduled along with a breakfast, lunch or dinner.

#7 Start a dinner club

This is a great idea that works. It helps to have a teaching institution in your area, but it can work without one as well. Gather a list of your target doctors. As you read over your list, separate those whose professional politics might exclude them from being together. Make two if you have to, but try to stick with one at a time. They should be similar in age and have the same or related specialty as you. The members may or may not be your customers. Either is fine and you should also include current fellows if possible.

The object is to have quarterly dinners at a very nice restaurant. It will start small, but over time it can grow into a very powerful group of doctors for you.

They will know what you are selling, but you should rarely, if ever, discuss product specific business unless they bring it up. And if you are asked, do not talk about it long until you change the subject. Allow the group to form a bond with you in a friendly environment. Here is what you can get out of it:

- You will belong to their group, not simply be another rep
- Just by being the initiator, they will eventually talk about your products
- Any solid customer will become a spokesman for you when you are gone
- You will be viewed as a resource, even if you only pay for the meal
- Your access to them (in the OR, etc.) will be greatly increased
- Ultimately, you will generate more business

You can even invite some club members' referring doctors to join your group from time to time. It is a great business opportunity for your club members to interact with their referrals at your meetings. You can also bring in outside consultants like medical malpractice experts, financial analysts, etc. So long as their attendance is free, you should not be in violation of any law. Check with your manager about your ideas first.

Other reps might try to get into your dinner group. DO NOT UNDER ANY CIRCUMSTANCES let anyone else in your group. Doing so will cause the group to dissolve faster than you can blink because the docs will think you are playing bait-and-switch. Keep the group true to your original purpose – reward and camaraderie.

#8 Start a patient support group

Starting a patient support group could produce a huge payback for you. If your product benefits a patient subset with a specific medical problem (most do), you can start a quarterly or semi-annual meeting in a specific town for those patients. You can even move it from town to town. Have fun and implement your own ideas.

Many patients love to gather and discuss their specific problems with other community members who have the same experiences. They can share fears, joys and success stories among the group.

The way to get the payoff is by inviting a specialist (a doctor or a nurse) to answer their questions. The specialists will be somewhat indebted to you for helping them reach out to the community and expand their business.

To sell the idea to the doctors, present the support group as a way to generate referrals and new business for their practice. You can even set it up in a nearby town in which the doctor does not have business, but wants to target.

There is probably already a local support group for most common ailments. Contact the local branch of these organizations first. They might be able to completely plan and advertise your event. Help them, and they will help you.

#9 When a new doctor is coming into your territory

If you hear that a new doctor is coming into your area, take action immediately. Contact your rep counterpart in the doctor's hometown. Find out everything you can about product choices, styles and most importantly, the state of the relationship between your company and the doctor.

Regardless of the relationship, **you** must try to contact this new customer **in person** and **before** they move into your territory. The perfect scenario would be to have dinner with the doctor, your manager and the doctor's current rep before the move. Assume that your competitors are trying to set up this meeting as well (especially after this book has been out a few years).

Even if you only make the offer, your efforts are not wasted. We have practiced this for years and picked up new customers **simply by making the offer**. Offers to dinner, symposiums, etc. are sometimes as powerful as actually getting customers to go.

If setting up this meeting is too difficult, there is something else you can do. This only works if the doctor and the former rep have had a good relationship. After the new doctor arrives, fly the former rep into your town for a dinner with the doc. This might be the difference between keeping a customer and losing one.

#10 How to introduce a landmark new product

This concept can easily save or cost you $1,000,000. If you introduce your product incorrectly, it could cost much more.

Assume that your company is about to hit the market with a great new product – in limited supply. This happens all the time in the medical community. Who are you going to give it to first? You have two choices and companies often select the wrong one.

The first option is to try to maximize total sales volume by taking the new product to the biggest volume opportunity. This appears to make sense both on paper and from a strategic standpoint. Careful, this is not necessarily the case.

Big, quick sales increases make the company happy, but think in terms of *at least* the next 12 to 18 months. There is more involved than short-term gains. We have seen a product launch that was done incorrectly and cost the company at least $250,000,000! That is a quarter of a billion dollars ... at least. What a mistake. All because they wanted the big, quick hit and did not look at the long term.

First consider this. If this large volume opportunity is <u>not a current customer</u>, you risk alienating yourself from current customers who *are* purchasing from you today. These are also the people whose sales funded the research and development or acquisition capital responsible for the new product. You might make large gains today, but it can cause serious pain when a competitor finally hits the market. And there is always competition sooner or later.

Then you get hit with a double whammy. It is an absolute possibility you will lose your newfound customers when a competitor comes out with a similar product. Your old base of customers, whom you upset by not bringing the new product to them, might enjoy making a statement by switching to your competitor. Now where are you?

The second option we like much better. That is to take new products to your current list of customers. You must reward them for their loyalty to you, your product and your company. If you take your new products elsewhere, we do not blame your doctors for thinking their business is not important to you. Like we said before, doctors love to prove a point. So prove to them they made the right decision by partnering with you and your company.

#11 You get the "I'm upset with you" phone call

We all upset someone in this business at some point. Sooner or later it will happen to you, if it has not happened already. There is no sense in talking about all the different ways you can mess up. The list would go on forever. When this happens, no matter where you are, or what you are doing, drop everything. Go visit this customer **in person** immediately. Whether you are right or wrong in what you did is not the point. Your explanation or apology is better received face to face instead of on the phone. Allowing your customer to look into your eyes is very important and should not be minimized.

The customer should appreciate that you cared enough to make the contact in person. You should also consider this strategy if you get cross with a colleague within your company. Contact them in person, work out the problem and make them feel important. Your career is too important to let a mild scuffle escalate into something more.

#12 Write down any important agreements

Here is one lesson we learned the hard way. We would never have expected this to fall into the million-dollar category. In fact, it was on the $100,000 list and was moved up after this event. Here is what happened.

A hospital and our company agreed to take back (or exchange) some product of ours they no longer used. In order to grow our business (and pay for the swap), we agreed to exchange these goods for products they currently purchased from a competitor. Our efforts would save the hospital about $20,000. We were very specific in the products, which were part of the swap — or so we thought.

Six months later, the customer demanded credit for every item they were buying from us. Under our agreement only specific items were part of the exchange. We came up with a copy of the agreement in writing, but it did not matter. Our integrity was questioned, and we ended up losing every product we sold in the hospital.

This problem is avoided by taking notes **while** cutting "deals." Even informal notes taken during your deliberations are all you need. When an agreement is made, show the customer your notes and go over them together. Make sure you are both in agreement. Then make a copy of the notes (preferably before you leave) for your customer. Your contract department should write up something formal from your notes. Present a copy to your customer for their files.

Take notes while cutting deals.

#13 The power of Saturday

We promised to show you how to eliminate every gatekeeper between you and your customers. Here it is. This idea is valuable but should not be used all of the time. Hospitals are open 24 hours a day, seven days a week. Purchasing managers, materials departments and office staffs work only five days a week. You can probably see where we are heading. Most all doctors now work on Saturdays. They at least make rounds in the morning. Many perform cases. In other words, the hospital is open for business on Saturday (and even Sunday).

Be careful about working on Saturday. Some doctors will inevitably view it as an infringement on their personal time. You should know how a doctor will receive you before you attempt this. Do not try it unless you *know* the outcome will be positive.

Another group of doctors will regard your effort as taking the extra step to earn their business. These are the doctors to attack with Saturday meetings. Even if you do not make a sales presentation, just bringing in breakfast or lunch is an unusual treat for the weekend workers. Reading the newspaper in the operating room lounge (for example), will be a nice showing for you. Also, the possibility exists for the nurses or techs to talk about the fact you were there even if the doc does not show.

We have never known a manager to care if you drop work one day of the week and exchange it for a Saturday. In fact, many top managers could care less how you spend your time — as long as your numbers are good. How you generated your sales numbers should be secondary to the fact you are generating good ones.

#14 Another note about hospital hours

We have one particular friend who constantly churned out great sales years. We sat in amazement at his staggering sales numbers. He was top three in the country every year. None of us thought he was overtly smart either. We knew he was doing something differently.

As all good sales reps do, he made special efforts to call on every department that used his products. This is how he differentiated himself: He called on them in the middle of the night! He would always bring a snack, pens, etc. He showed up with no appointments. Most nurses who work the nightshift do not know what to do when someone in a suit shows up, especially someone with goodies. They listened to every pitch he threw. Then, they would ask for his products.

These customers are equally as important as the ones who receive normal billing during daylight hours. The difference was no one else called on these people. No one! If you consider the many departments that run three seven-hour shifts, it is possible the daytime shift is the only one garnering any attention. Therefore, you might be leaving 66 percent of your customers out of the decision making process. Consider your business and your customers when deciding if the midnight runs are right for you.

#15 Become a networking magnet

It is important to become a networking machine. There is no exception in the medical and pharmaceutical field. Your first goal should be to meet one new person every day or five new people per week. Add each one of these people to your PDA for life. With new filing and storing methods of PDA devices, there is never a need to eliminate names. When a contact moves on, move their name to an archive folder. You never know when a name from your past will resurface.

Find new ways to leverage every relationship you can. Here is yet another great tip that has worked time and time again. **Know which customers are friends with each other**. If you are the current supplier to one of those friends, use their relationship for your gain. Use this technique with physician partners in a medical group as well.

Here is the example. Doctor A (or customer A) is friends with Doctor B. Doctor A use your products and you two have a good relationship. Doctor B docs not use your products. Invite both doctors to dinner at your expense.

Do not use this time to sell your products. In fact, it is better not to bring up sales talk at all. They both know who you are and ultimately why you are there. They will eventually talk between themselves about your product. This is a silent process, but it builds a strong rapport among the three of you. Your access to Doctor B is increased as well, so you can talk products later.

#16 Have monthly lunch meetings with your fellow reps

If you are not currently meeting once a month with the local reps you work with, it is a mistake. If your company is not paying for this meeting, it is a mistake. Every person who works for your company (regardless of product line or division) and who covers the same territory should meet monthly.

Even if there are only two of you, meeting monthly doubles your eyes and ears in the territory. If there are 30 reps, so be it. Reserve a large area. These individuals cover similar areas, have good account knowledge and are on the same team!

We have conducted meetings like these for years. Every time these meetings conclude, great information has been shared. We can even recall a single case where the company picked up a half-million dollar contract from an idea that originated at a monthly luncheon. If the company decides not to pick up the tab for lunch, invite a local manager and see if they will pick it up. We think it is foolish not to do so.

#17 Find the renegade or rebel

This is one of your author's (Jack) favorite techniques and one he has used it with great success since the late 1960s. It is equally potent today. Remember the power of the renegade or the rebel. There is no faster way to sell products than to identify this person. The rebel has the following traits:

- He/she is extremely outgoing and boisterous.

- He/she is willing to tell others his/her opinions.

- He/she is willing to explain his/her opinions.

- He/she does not care what anyone else is doing.

There is more we could add, but you get the general idea. Having a rebel use your products can be an absolute goldmine. If your rebels are powerful, they can change the usage patterns of an entire hospital. More than just a key decision maker – the rebel is a decision maker *with attitude*!

No matter how many or how few customers you have, **there are always rebels among them.** You might consider that your primary job in sales is to hunt the rebel.

If you are working with doctors, finding the rebel is actually easy. Just ask the ancillary staff which ones are most vocal about the products they use. Bump these doctors up on your list of targets. **If they already use you, check their willingness to speak on your behalf (during your programs).** Their conviction will shine and convince other customers your products are viable.

#18 Own a voice recorder of some sort

Is this a million dollar idea? You bet. Sales reps and managers spend an incredible amount of time traveling. Most of it in a car or airplane. Simply having a digital voice recorder available makes your brain function differently. Ideas **will** start coming to you. We promise. If you have no method of recording these ideas, they are forgotten quickly. The ideas will vary from presentations to doctors, accounts that need attention or any number of other topics. Having the ability to quickly save your thoughts and ideas for later use is paramount to your efficiency.

Many new PDA's have a built-in voice recorder on them (as well as the ability to run files from Power Point, Excel, Word, MP3, etc.) If you are looking to purchase a PDA anyway, get one with all the bells and whistles and learn to use it. If you use your voice recorder immediately, you will see some amazing results. In fact, it might become as important as your cell phone. It is not uncommon for me to come back from a one-day business trip with 10 to 25 new messages. One of them might even grow your business by $1,000,000!

"No idea will impact your business if you don't remember it."

—Ryan Gray

#19 Falling on you sword without getting killed

There are many ways to fall on your sword for a customer. What we mean by this is being in the unenviable position of choosing one customer over another. The preference is obvious. Do not get into this position. Unfortunately, you will find yourself making these choices from time to time. We will give you two true examples to illustrate our point.

The subject of sole-source contracts arose during a recent conversation between a rep and an operating room coordinator. The coordinator was not interested in any contract that required a single supplier. She did not want to upset her doctors and eliminate their choices. She asked the rep not to approach the subject with anyone else. The rep agreed.

About a month later, a purchasing manager called the rep for an appointment. At the appointment, she requested a sole-source bid from the company for the hospital. The rep stayed true to his commitment and informed the purchasing manager of his promise to the operating room coordinator.

The rep and the purchasing manager agreed the two departments (purchasing and the operating room) would talk, and the hospital would contact the rep when needed. All was quiet for another two months.

At this time, a doctor pulled the rep aside after a case. He stated his concern that the rep might lose the hospital's business to a competitor. The competitor had offered the hospital a very low price for a sole-source contract. To make matters worse, the purchasing manager told the doctor that the rep was arrogant for not offering this type of contract. Now he was stuck in a totally defensive position with several people in the hospital.

There are several very valuable lessons to learn from this scenario. First, **never assume two people will discuss an issue together, even if they say they will**. It was ultimately the rep's responsibility to coordinate the proper communication. Second, **respond to every request made by any customer**. Fulfill the request and personally notify anyone else who might be involved.

In this case, the rep should have offered the sole source contract, then notified the OR supervisor of that action.

Here's another example of a rep falling on a sword, but gaining a fallback position. A colleague of ours spent years building a very nice pacemaker territory. He "owned" a few busy doctors who used him on every case. At one point, a new specialist joined their practice. On occasion, his regular doctors would refer patients to this new specialist. The rep noticed the specialist began putting <u>his</u> name on patient follow-up forms instead of the referring doc. These patients should have remained in the permanent care of the referring doctor.

My friend pointed this out to his doctors and the specialist. In essence, he placed himself in the middle of the situation. By calling out the specialist publicly, he eliminated any future business the specialist might give him.

This is a prime example of falling on a sword for your customers. Here was his fallback position. The doctors whom he stood up for remained loyal. They continue to give him plenty of business. The problem is the rep greatly reduced his ability to grow his territory. Actually, this whole situation could have been avoided by taking the discrepancy to the doctors and letting them confront the specialist.

Explore all other alternatives diligently before falling on a sword for anyone.

#20 Know how often your customers see your competitors

Build a frame of reference in regard to how often your customers see your competitors. Gathering this information might be harder than you realize. You might have 30 to 100 accounts multiplied by as many as 10 competitors.

First, apply the 80-20 rule. Focus on those accounts you cannot afford to lose or those accounts currently on your target list. There are several ways to find out how often a competitor is around. Many hospitals have rep sign-in books that can be easily accessed. *Take your time when signing in.* Peruse as many pages as you feel comfortable doing. No one will likely comment. The other way is to simply ask around.

We do not want our competitors in front of our customers more than we are. The goal should be a minimum of equal time. This trick can also help us with time management. If you are running three or four visits to one by your competitor, and you have all the business, you might be able to drop back by a visit. Add this visit to one of your other targets. Be aware this is an ever-flowing correlation, and we must be able to act quickly in either direction.

#21 Immediate follow-up

One of the most annoying traits anyone can have is poor follow-up. We experience it consistently in every area of our lives. Call the phone company and see how long it takes them to return your call. Fortunately for them, our options are limited or they would be forced to change. Customers in the medical arena have more options than they can realistically consider.

Even within your own corporation, you will be astonished with the amount of slow follow-up. Marketing, customer service and management should all strive to deliver responses in a timely manner. Topnotch reps know we cannot afford to neglect our follow-up.

If you make a promise to a customer or co-worker, you should complete that action within 24 hours. At the very least, they should know you are working on it. Communicate in some manner to show you remember the promise. Our goal is to answer your e-mail questions to our website the day they are asked.

When we make a promise as a medical rep, we try to fulfill the action *before we leave the customer's office.* This is highly probable if we can solve the issue with one phone call. For example, if a customer wants product literature, make the phone call and fill the request from that customer's office. Not only does this guarantee the promise is kept, but if the literature does *not* arrive, you are not blamed by your customer.

You rarely forget action items when you fulfill them immediately.

#22 Your mental ax

Be willing to sharpen your mental ax on a consistent basis. This industry provides more information than you can ever absorb. New journal articles, clinical books and clinical studies are published daily. If you are not constantly working on your clinical schooling you are missing out. Try to read all relevant information that pertains to your specialty. By striving for clinical excellence, your customers will start to view you as a viable source of information. You never know when a seemingly innocent answer you give to a customer will literally save someone's life. When that happens, you have gained a customer for life.

There are also clinical certifications and courses available to you as a rep. Taking one of these courses or a clinical certification exam is a great idea. They force you to study clinical issues. They also prove your proficiency to your customers. And your company knows you are serious about developing your skills. Having these extra skills is great to bring up at promotion time.

#23 Temperance

We have provided over 20 actionable items that can create $1,000,000 in sales for your company and will increase your commissions significantly. What you also need is temperance. Temperance is defined by Webster as "moderation in action, thought, or feeling: Restraint."

C.S. Lewis probably defined it better for our purpose by saying, "*Go the right distance and no further or shorter*".

In the medical and pharmaceutical world, it is possible to work 24 hours a day, seven days a week. You must have sensed that possibility as you read this text. No company or territory position should promote an insane lifestyle. We have seen sales jobs destroy families with ridiculously high on-the-job hours. No job or money is worth that price. For this reason, you must practice temperance with regard to your career and find the right balance for you and your family. If you work for a company or manager who does not share this belief, consider finding new work. No one should be required to work 80 hours every week. You will be happier and more productive if you strive to achieve proper temperance.

Working hard can produce nothing. Working smart can produce anything.

22 More $1,000,000 ideas exclusive to the MSDR: Corporate Edition

#24 Get them while they are young

We cannot say enough about the power of building relationships with fellows and residents in your field. Some of the biggest companies have made an absolute living out of cultivating and training these young doctors on their products. This concept will not deliver $1 million this year. But it is worth 10 times that in the future.

First we need to cover the corporate side. Corporations at the minimum should have programs set aside every year just for residents. These events should take place over several days either at the home office, or in nice locations. Well-recognized speakers should be brought in to cover various topics of interest. In other words, the red carpet should be rolled out.

As individuals, know that your competitors are actively trying to build relationships with the doctors who will soon be in private practice. If you are not spending equal time between these doctors and your current customers, we feel you are making a mistake. This concept even goes back to biblical teachings. The saying goes, "Train up a child in the way he should go and when he is old he will not depart from it."

The same principle applies with our doctors. How many times have we heard, "I trained on that product, and I'm staying with it until it fails me." It is always easier to shape the thoughts of physicians early in their career.

#25 Getting to the hospital very early

Getting to the hospital very early in the day has numerous advantages. First, many of the gatekeepers have not shown up for work. This increases your access to key people you are trying to talk to. There is another group of people who have probably not shown up early either…your competitors.

Any time you get a quick face to face with a customer, even if you don't get the chance to talk for long, you implant a subliminal advertising piece in their mind. That doctor will unknowingly think about you during the day when they make a choice in product selection.

We guarantee it. (If it didn't work, we wouldn't know what the word "billboard" meant.)

You get an additional advantage in that the doctors' minds are fresh. They have not been bombarded with patient problems, scheduling problems or other detrimental events. You do not even have to sell anything to benefit greatly. In most cases, doctors know why we are there.

Vendesi Group senior adviser Jack Erickson had just finished the year as the number two sales representative in the country. But Jack had a problem. He wanted to be number one. Jack lived in the Central time zone, while the number one rep lived on Eastern time. Jack began working the new year on Eastern time. He wanted his day to start the same time as the number one rep. He reaped the benefits of being the early bird and the following year, Jack was back at number one.

#26 Specialty clothing

Many hospitals today have scrubs or casual clothing displaying their hospital logo. Finding out if these things are available can make a lot of sense. You'll notice a difference in some of these following areas:

- Higher-quality "mirroring" (looking like your customer)
- Increased level of access
- Less likely to be hassled by a gatekeeper
- Showing support for their organization

You can have scrubs made, t-shirts, golf shirts and more! You do not have to be over the top, but just give a subtle message of support to the hospital and the staff. These are just a few of the benefits of wearing specialty clothing. You never know when you can get past one individual who will lead you to a new sale.

#27 Thank-you notes

One of the most overlooked power tools in business is a thank-you note. From new sales reps to your CEO, everyone should write thank-you notes. These notes should be handwritten by the sender on either personal or company letterhead. We prefer personal, professional note cards with your name engraved on the inside. Personal note cards relay a sense of individual appreciation as opposed to corporate appreciation.

As a field sales rep, you should probably write handwritten thank-you letters any time you spend quality time with a doctor (or important customer). If a doctor stops by and has lunch with you, you should definitely write them a handwritten thank you. Also, strongly consider writing a thank you to any office manager who arranges a sales presentation, lunch or dinner for you.

Attention upper-level managers and executives: You are not exempt from writing thank-you notes. Some top CEOs spend the first five minutes of EVERY DAY writing handwritten thank-you notes to customers, employees and other outside entities. It is a good practice that will absolutely help get things done.

"People work hardest for those who appreciate them."
—Ryan Gray

#28 Car time can be valuable

We believe that at least 25 percent of your travel time should be in silence. Meaning, you should not always have music, the radio or a telephone sending messages to your mind. You will be amazed how much information is brought to your conscious mind when there is no outside interference competing for brainwaves. You will think of new ideas, strategies or to do items if you give this a shot.

Ben Franklin has silence listed as one of his 13 virtues of life. If it is good enough for Ben, it is good enough for us. It is so hard for us to achieve any level of silence in our lives that the car can be our last bastion of peace. For those of you who are interested, Ben's other 12 virtues are:

Temperance	Order
Resolution	Frugality
Industry	Sincerity
Justice	Moderation
Cleanliness	Tranquility
Chastity	Humility

#29 Why marketing messages collapse and how to avoid the fall

Envision this. A group of experts sit around for months pouring over statistics, charts, graphs and clinical papers. From somewhere pops out a unique and splendid idea. A convergence of mind and thought that produces something so revolutionary, people are sure to embrace it, believe it and act on it. This idea has now taken flight and nothing will stop it from being a catalyst for the product it represents.

Marketing analysts prepare and fix every detail of the message. Editors check for errors, rework the material and meet with printers. The printing company is paid overtime to complete the campaign early. The sales force is flown in for a midweek conference to discuss the new message and the plan for its delivery. Everyone is excited to get the message out to their customers and create a buzz in the industry that will create a new stream of sales dollars to the company and commissions into their pockets.

Then, two days later: The marketing piece is stuck in a file box in the rep's trunk. It will never see the light of day again.

Does this sound familiar? Millions of dollars are wasted every year because there is a fundamental breakdown between the marketing department and the street. There are some companies out there that absolutely know how to get a message to their customers. It is like a tidal wave across the country. I've personally sold against some of the best. It seemed like every doctor in the territory could spout off the same, predetermined objections. How did they do it? The answer is both simple and complex.

1. It starts with a simple message. I've seen some of the most confusing marketing pieces imaginable. How these ever were approved and produced is beyond belief. Whether we are making marketing pieces or making a simple sales call, you must know the specific message you want the prospect to hear. Once you have your message, reduce it to a few sentences. Then make it even smaller. The very best selling messages in the world are only a few words. Take Volvo as an illustration. Their entire message

is one word — "safety". No one owns that position better than Volvo. As an added benefit, customers are skeptical if another car manufacturer implies a Volvo is not safe.

So, have one simple message to deliver at a time. Make sure the core of the message can be easily given in only half a minute. Drive it home until your customers know it instinctively. Keith Reinhard, Chairman of DDB once said, "If you can't write your strategy or idea on the back of a business card, it's too complex to execute."

2. Have a specific target list of customers you want to receive the message. This step is quite easy for any medical or pharmaceutical supply company today. When you consider how many representatives you might have in the field, getting your message out to your targets can probably be completed in a matter of days.

3. A conversation must take place with the messengers. There is only one of two paths a company can take. You must either incentivize the reps with monetary rewards for delivering the message to their list or carefully explain the benefits of delivering the message.

The first option is easy to understand. The second might be the most powerful, but it requires more work. Comprehensive sales professionals should understand the ultimate payback for delivering specific sales messages to their customers. They should also instinctively know these messages are tailored to influence their customers to purchase or purchase more of their products. Good sales representatives should know all these things. It is our experience, however, that many representatives completely gloss over the delivery of messages. If that occurs, you will know the breakdown was in this step.

4. Finally you must have a system to track your results. Most companies look at sales results both prior to the marketing release and after the release. This is their sole basis for evaluating the success or failure of a marketing campaign. We believe that an entire piece is being left out. Companies should look at message deliveries first. Then let the bottom line follow.

Here is what we mean by "message deliveries". If a sales representative has 50 customers, he or she is responsible for 50 documented message deliveries. Each company can define its own terms, but the point is to have every customer actually receive the marketing message, know when the delivery was made and track those deliveries.

The company can then spend as much time as they want tracking the effectiveness of the campaign because each stage was properly acted upon.

Using effective campaign management allows us to answer another question. Why do reps place every marketing piece the company has ever created in the trunk of their car? Are they waiting for someone to ask you for it? No one knows it is in there! I laugh at myself because I did this for years. Now I carry two copies as reference in a folder that is product specific. (We cover how to effectively disburse these marketing pieces in the previous section.)

#30 Quality regional meetings

It is true that the more communication you have amongst your group, the more ideas will be shared. It is also true that we live in a world of conference calls, e-mail and voice mail. These mediums are not the optimal venue for effective idea sharing and collaboration. Members of any group are not as attentive, engaged or responsive at electronic meetings as they are in person.

Meeting participants are most likely to introduce ideas and become an active participant in a small group setting. It is for this reason that companies should have quarterly meetings to allow this kind of interaction between their sales reps. No matter what topics are on the agenda, make sure there is ample time set aside for the general sharing of ideas.

These meetings can be costly, so frequency should be handled accordingly. Nonetheless, great ideas will be shared, the experience level of the group will rise and sales will go up after this kind of meeting.

#31 Reward your best customers

Great customers are hard to come by. They are sometimes hard to keep as well. Make your life easier by giving them a reward for using you. We think a great way to reward them is with an award. Specifically implant awards. These awards commemorate implant/usage milestones of your customers. For instance, if doctors implant 100 pacemakers they should be recognized. Then they should be recognized again at 200.

You will have to come up with logical numbers depending on your product. Here is a good rule of thumb. They should be earned about every 24 months by your very BEST customers. Anything more is too much. Know that some award levels will be unattainable by some customers.

What kind of award should you give? The answer is highly dependent on your personality and that of your company. Shadowboxes with your product in them and a plaque noting the accomplishments are always good. There are many areas of gray in regards to what constitutes a gift and what is a device demo. Check with your manager or legal department about your award.

REPS: If your company does not give out these awards, do it yourself. Never depend on anyone else for your economic future.

#32 The ears of the hospital are upon you

The following is a true story that might have cost this sales rep millions in business. The story is so basic that over 90 percent of the people we talk to about it respond with, "I never even thought about that."

Recognize the fact that there are people all over the hospital that might be able to hear a conversation you are having. Most people are somewhat discrete until they get on their phone. This is what happened to one such rep who was on the phone in an elevator.

She was riding with me and had no idea who I might be. Frankly, I didn't care whom she was talking to. She piqued my interest when she started talking about a hospital bid for a very specific product. She proceeded to talk about dollar amounts of their bid, hospital usage and even the timeframe for delivering the bid to the hospital. Under most circumstances, she might have been safe. Not this time. She was a direct competitor of a lifelong friend of mine.

After I got in the car, it took about a minute to get my friend on the phone. He now knew everything about that competitive bid. That would be like having the opposing teams playbook and game plan before the game! I don't know what happened, but the bid was for well into seven figures.

#33 Own the outlying areas

Everyone calls on the big hospitals and large volume doctors. We are here to tell you that is exactly what you should do as well. But here is something else sales people need to do. Own the outlying areas of their territory. Their cumulative worth can be many times more than your largest account. These customers are generally sold to less often than larger ones. Generally, if you pay even decent attention to them, you can earn their business.

We are not advocating spending excess amounts of time calling on these people. Check your target list and compare that to the time it will take to add these accounts. We are saying to make a conscious decision to pick up their business. There may even be more sales potential than you realized.

#34 Get involved with the community

If you know anything about Vendesi Group, you know we are very involved with charitable organizations across the country as well as in our own community. We are all called to contribute. We also contribute to different causes for different reasons.

There's no reason we cannot involve ourselves with community work within our hospitals. Most hospitals have several charity events throughout the year. Traditionally, companies have taken part in these events with monetary contributions. We believe sales reps should do more. Specifically, work at or for the event. There are many tasks to be completed at any event and volunteers are always needed to complete these tasks.

Treat time spent working on this event as your sales time. Your work benefits at least four groups of people: The hospital, the recipient of the charity work, your company and you are all rewarded for their involvement.

This principle is at the heart of being viewed as more than just a sales rep in the eyes of our customer. That is your ultimate goal. Besides, it is the right thing to do.

#35 Make your relationships yours

You worked long and hard to build personal relationships with your customers. It might sound selfish, but do not share those relationships with anyone unless they work for your company <u>or</u> you know for sure that both of you will benefit. The following example may better clarify this point.

Another sales rep comes to you and says, "You have a great relationship with Dr. Smith. I'm really trying to get to know him better. Do you mind if I come play golf with you two sometime?"

You can answer whatever you like but know this: This rep does not have a relationship with Dr. Smith. If he did, he would not need you to set this meeting. Number two is this: Dr. Smith probably is not using his products. **There might be a good reason for it, and the rep will probably not share that information with you.** That reason may be personal, product related or company related. Whatever the reason is, it could be transferred to you. Think long and hard before you share your relationships.

Of course there is another hand. You should probably consider using this tactic in reverse whenever you get the chance. Riding the coattails of someone else's great relationship makes your job much easier. You might even advance your personal rapport with this customer by years with only one visit. This is a very powerful tactic. Just don't let it be used to your detriment.

#36 The most powerful sales question

For every list there can only be one number one, one most powerful or one best. For us the selection of the most powerful sales question in the world was easy. You can ultimately be the judge for yourself. Here it is.

"What would you do if you were me?"

You can ask this question at numerous points in a sales call or sales cycle. Their answer will give you a roadmap to follow with your given prospect. It is also powerful because it is a hard question not to answer. We believe most prospects prefer not to answer questions directly, or they flat-out lie. The only answer you don't want to hear is, "nothing different".

We think the best time to use this question is during your close. After everything has been discussed and you are awaiting an answer, use this question, and then just wait. More often than not, your prospects will start the closing process all by themselves. You are simply using this as a trigger to say, "I'm done, now let's get on with it."

#37 Keep every customer in the loop

Sometimes the sales process can drag on forever at a hospital. It is hard to remember who we talked to and what messages we delivered. Our customers forget these things faster than we do. It is our responsibility to swing through and talk to everyone who is involved in a decision at regular intervals.

We heard of the following mistake that cost a sales rep business. The sales rep was selling capital equipment and had worked on a large account for months. He initially made sales calls to everyone involved in the process. He was getting bogged down in the medical units of the hospital. People continued to refer him to others and no one was willing to make a decision.

During this time, he inadvertently stopped calling on the purchasing manager. The purchasing manager had a deadline for capital equipment submission that the rep never knew about. By the time an agreement was made by the nursing staff, it was too late for the order to be placed. This could have been avoided by keeping everyone involved in the process.

#38 Excuse yourself

If you are around medical sales long enough, the following is bound to happen. One of your customers will perform surgery on someone you know personally. You must excuse yourself from the case. No real good can come from it, and you could possibly get yourself into some real trouble.

Imagine if the case goes south. Now, you are either culpable as a participant or a witness in possible litigation. Neither one is good. So the situation is best avoided.

On a similar note, let's talk about referring friends and family to your doctors/customers. Just one word of advice, be positive. Talk about good doctors and good hospitals. Refrain from talking about bad doctors and bad hospitals. Your friends or family *could* repeat anything you say in front of their doctor or nurse. You might be taking a huge risk.

#39 Your competitor's bid is...

What do you do when a customer tells you the exact price of your competitors bid? One of two things is happening. Unless this is a personal friend, it is probably number two.

1. The customer wants you to get the business. For any number of reasons, this person is doing you a favor. Take the information, say thanks, and then try to figure out why it was given to you. You do not want to overlook a favor, but you do not want to be taken for a ride either. Proceed with caution.

2. Option two is the most likely. The person who shared the bids with you is also sharing your bid information with your competitors. The goal is to get you in a bidding war against each other. This is a shrewd, probably unethical (and in some cases illegal) business practice that some people will use.

The purpose of this idea is to show you that everyone you meet is dealing with you from a personal point of view. Their own personal interests (usually financial ones) will always be at the center of their actions. So proceed with caution.

#40 Your mirror

Numbers 40 and 41 really go together. Number 40 revolves around the idea that people notice you whether you know it or not. Most of the time, it is not someone who can make a difference in your business. Sometimes, however, it will be.

We should all try to be extra courteous around hospitals and doctor's offices. Open doors for others, step off elevators if there is not enough room or pick up loose trash that might have fallen on the floor. If you are always in too big of a hurry to take action on these fine points, you are missing out.

Even if others never notice it, you will know it and feel good about yourself. Von Goethe said, "A man's manners are a mirror in which he shows his portrait." Be all that you were meant to be. Your personal satisfaction and possibly career will both be improved.

#41 Your reputation

What is your number one asset as a rep? Your reputation. Do whatever it takes to protect it. Once it is gone, it is most likely gone forever. We cover some personal things to avoid in other areas of this book. But rest assured, your reputation is worth millions of dollars to you in this marketplace.

There are many sales reps who are dishonest in different areas of their business. I will also wager that sooner or later all of them will be "discovered" by their customers. In fact, their customers probably already know it. Ultimately, dishonest reps will become the last option to customers when they are deciding on a product or service.

#42 Hang out with the company's winners

According to Earl Nightingale, we all conform to outside groups. It is impossible to be a complete individual. Someone somewhere has already done just about everything. This is certainly true in the pure sense of selling. Nightingale says that instead of conforming to the people who are losing, we should conform (emulate) those people who are winning. Or simply put, hang out with the best sales people you can find.

To be more specific, conform to the top 5 percent of all wage earners. If you look at your territory as your business, you should be able to pull the best practices and habits of successful people in any business. Don't limit yourself to only what others in medical sales are doing that is successful. Look at influential people like Harvey MacKay, Jerry Jones, even Donald Trump (just don't emulate the hair.) Think big and you will be big.

"If you walk with the lame, you will learn to limp."
—Henry R. Hillenmeyer

#43 Don't feed the janitor

We are sorry to say this, and yes, we know the janitor needs to eat, but medical supply and pharmaceutical companies are feeding too many people. We all need to step back and gauge the effectiveness of our "meals programs". Customers have also grown used to our goodwill, and some take advantage of us. Some customers are even sick of the whole thing and have banned lunches altogether.

Everyone gets stuck some times. I've personally fed a security guard. How did that happen? Our goal is to be conscious of our target audience and the message we want to deliver. If bringing in food will help deliver that message to our targeted customer, so be it. If we are feeding the world and delivering no messages, we are missing out and wasting money.

If you are interested in gauging the effectiveness of your lunches, try going cold turkey for a month. See what it does for your business or your access at your accounts. Everyone is probably more effective if they do fewer, but targeted, lunches.

#44 While on the topic of food, how to host a great dinner

No one loves hosting a great dinner more than we do. To make it memorable for your guests, there are just a few things you should absolutely do.

1. First and foremost, work with a restaurant that is known for hosting great dinner presentations. They should have a corporate accounts representative and know what an overhead projector is (and why you need an outlet for it!) The more dinner programs they put on, the better service you will receive.

2. Most people prepare seating based on the maximum number of people they think will arrive. What this usually leads to is empty place settings. In order to make your dinner appear well attended, do the opposite. Have a room big enough for all contingencies, but only make place settings for those people you actually know are going to attend. Then, have a plan for the restaurant staff to add seating quickly as it becomes necessary. Your guests receive a silent message, technically called "social acceptance". The message is your program is popular and the topic must be good because they have to add more seating. On the flip side, a room with a

bunch of empty seats doesn't say much for your program, your company or your speaker.

3. Pick a great speaker.

4. Pick a great wine. It makes the evening more memorable. You can even get the sommelier to do a wine presentation for a better effect.

#45 BONUS: for ex-clinical representatives

This is specifically for those sales reps who used to be clinicians, nurses, PAs or the like. **You no longer are employed by the hospital.** You now work for, and are under the liability of, your company. While you are working, do not do **<u>anything</u>** you used to do when you were a clinician. Do not pick up patients, answer ringing telephones or touch medications or equipment. We know it is a hard habit to break, but you must.

We are quite certain your new company feels the same way. If something were to ever go wrong with a patient you were "helping" you could be liable. Save yourself the headache and enjoy your new role as an observer.

Some $100,000 Ideas as Well

While some of these ideas are probably not $1,000,000 ideas, they should not go untold. Used correctly, they have power, and they are used by many top reps. In fact, when considered over the long term, they could easily be in the million-dollar category.

#46 Entertainment budgets

Budgets for entertainment are usually set by the joint efforts of management and accounting. Much time and consideration is spent reflecting the overall desires and values of your company. Striking a proper balance is more art than science.

What you as the rep should know is this: You should know the exact budgeted dollars allotted to you for entertainment purposes. Why? So you can spend every dime of it! If entertaining customers (legally) did not work, your budget for this would be $0. Companies know that spending time with customers is the key to building relationships and driving territory growth.

Use every penny allotted to you, and your business will increase.

#47 Walk through the hospital with a purpose

Walking through the hospital with purpose is *ultra* vital as it relates to access. If you walk briskly and with purpose through a department, the odds of someone stopping you are slim. We have found that even a slight pause while looking for directions can cause someone to ask you if you need help. Sometimes they are truly trying to help. More often they are checking to see if you belong or have business there.

Many people in the hospital *thoroughly* enjoy asking reps to leave their department or go to the purchasing department and "check in". They live for this power play. Do not slow down enough to give them the chance.

Walk like you know where you are going, and usually no one will bother you.

#48 Scrubs

How easy is it to point out a medical or pharmaceutical rep in a hospital? The answer is very easy. Ninety-nine percent of people wearing a suit in a hospital or a doctor's office are reps. Sometimes a $30 pair of scrubs will help you blend in and eliminate some gatekeepers. If all your competition wears a suit all the time, definitely get some scrubs! Be different and go either way when needed. At least try it to see what it does for you.

#49 Doctors are the ultimate power players

Ninety-five percent of the time a doctor will rule the roost when it comes to choice of medical devices and products. If you have a problem, do just what you do in real life. See a doctor. They call the shots. Try not to waste time giving sales pitches to those people who are not involved in the decision making process. Treat ancillary people with respect, but do not waste their time and yours. Using this technique allows you extra time to give sales presentations to good targets.

#50 If a doctor or customer gets irate with another employee

Some doctors lose it on a regular basis during a case. Some never do. There is a great surgeon that we refer to as "Ice Man." When he had an aorta disintegrate on him once during a procedure, his pulse did not go up a beat. He saved the patient as well.

The key point is if you happen to be present when a doctor is upset with someone in the room, dip out for a few minutes. You do not want your face visible when a doctor is pitching a fit. There is no need to be associated with the problem even at a subconscious level. Of course this point is moot if you are the one getting ripped... sorry.

Also, if you are making a sales call and the doc is having a terrible day, excuse yourself and come back. Not much will get accomplished in that environment anyway.

#51 If a customer starts bashing a competitor in front of you

From time to time, this is bound to happen to you. One of your customers will badmouth a competitor's products or services, or they might just rip them personally. It is really easy to pile on and say, "Yeah, you are right. They stink."

You must take the high road. Talking negatively about a competitor can only hurt you. And you should never talk bad about them personally. It **always** gets out. This is a mistake we made and paid for.

You do not have to tell everything you know. – Troy Compston

#52 How to change from a friend to a rep in one sentence

Here is a bit of Sales 101 for you that works regardless of your experience level. Making the transition from small talk to presenting your selling information can be delicate. The easiest way to make the change is to ask for permission. What a novel idea!

This can be done quite easily by asking the following question or something like it: "Do you mind if I put on my sales hat for a moment?" This alerts your prospect that product information is coming. You've also accomplished your goal in a non-threatening way. By asking for permission, they are more likely to listen to your information and provide real feedback.

Worth More than a Million!

Two things that can prolong your life!

Nutrition tips for sales representatives

We believe there are more important things than money, quite a few in fact. The first one included here is your body. Forget the "freshman 15." Working in the medical field can fatten you up more than that. Most of us cannot lose weight like we did at 18 either!

Constant travel, entertaining customers, standing all day and eating at restaurants can add weight in unwanted places and clog your arteries. I have asked a friend of mine, Jeff Toler, to write a quick guide to nutrition for the traveling sales rep. Jeff is a registered and licensed dietitian and an expert in the area. Take it away, Jeff.

Hello friends. It is a pleasure and honor to be asked by Vendesi Group to share my experiences with you. I have personally known some of their members for over 20 years. I believe you are receiving the best medical sales information available today.

I was asked to come up with some nutritional facts and tips for those people who travel, entertain and work long hours, sometimes without any breaks. It was my pleasure to be of assistance.

The first thing traveling sales representatives need to do is separate their normal life from work life. Think more like a person who works in an office environment with set hours. Getting into this mindset will make some of these suggestions easier to implement. Here they are:

1. *If you are bringing in bagels or donuts to a customer in the morning, eat breakfast at home first. If you do not have time, buy something for yourself that is low in fat at the same time you are making the purchase for your customers. Low fat is usually better than no fat. Many no-fat*

foods are full of sugar to make up for the lack of taste.

2. If you are ordering in lunch, make sure to order at least a small portion of low-fat foods. Even consider ordering up to half of your food from the low-fat menu. (You are usually placing the order anyway.) Your customers will thank you for it. You can also use Tip #1 for lunch.

3. Carry around a one-liter jug of water with you at all times. Try to empty it at least once per day. This will work to continually flush your body.

4. Eat until you are no longer hungry, not until you feel full.

5. Eat four times per day with breakfast being the most important.

6. Try to skip or limit alcoholic drinks before a meal.

7. When entertaining at night, try to eat fish and pork instead of red meat.

8. *If you want to take vitamin supplements make sure they have plenty of calcium and flaxseed.*

9. *Increase your physical activity, increase your sleep and decrease your level of stress.*

10. *LIVE HAPPY AND HEALTHY!*

I sincerely hope that you are successful in the workplace and maintain a good balance with your body. Treat it well, and it will be good to you. Thank you for allowing me the privilege of talking with you today. Best of luck.

Jeff Toler, R.D., L.D.

jeff_toler@yahoo.com

Basic hospital safety

This brief section is not complete enough for hospital or operating room personnel, but it should be useful to the average sales rep. These are a few ideas we learned through the years while working in labs and surgery suites. Even if you are a hands-on rep (meaning you are directly involved with the patient during the procedure), there are things you need to avoid. This is a liability issue as much as anything.

Do not touch anything. The phone can ring for 10 minutes, electric plugs can be falling out of the walls or an IV tube can be dangling in the doorway, but do not touch any of it. It is okay to point these things out to a circulator, but never handle them yourself. If you decide to answer a phone, you have no idea what you are getting in to. It is much better to stay out of the loop completely. Follow the simple rule that you are an observer, not an employee.

Wear protective glasses. Your company should probably allow you to expense such an item. If you work in a room where **anyone** is exposed to blood, you have the potential to be exposed as well. Over our career, we have been exposed by blood splash on several occasions. Most possible exposures are shielded from you with clear, protective eyewear. If you do not think this is important, try waiting 30 minutes for the patient's HIV test to come back. It is not fun.

The sterile field. The sterile field around a table goes from the edges of the table to the ceiling. Do not lean over the tables when showing your products. If you are frequently pointing things out on a sterile field, consider a laser-light pen. If you accidentally touch something sterile, *speak up immediately.* It is not uncommon for scrubbed technicians to accidentally bump something unsterile, including you. It is better to admit an accident than allow a patient to become infected.

These few ideas should keep you out of trouble while working around the patients. When in doubt you can ask for help.

How to Ruin Your Career Without Even Trying

"Foolish men imagine that because judgment for an evil thing is delayed, there is no justice."
—Thomas Carlyle

Expense report foolery

Expense report fraud by reps is hot on the minds of companies today. Fraudulent reporting is money straight off their bottom line. It seems so easy to write down extra expenses and pocket the money. The following example demonstrates this is not always the truth. And the consequences can be devastating.

Company A pays mileage to its employees. A particular employee writes off about 100 miles a day whether she actually drives it or not. What the heck, 100 miles a day is not out of the norm. Let us see.

500 miles x 4.5 weeks per month x 12 months = 26,000 miles

None of these numbers seems out of line. They might not be in a normal situation. This was not a normal situation. Her accounts were within a 15-mile radius of each other and her house. So the actual number of business miles she drove was about 13,000 per year. In three years she overstated her mileage by 39,000 miles. At $.39 per mile equals she totaled $15,200 in fraudulent expenses and tax evasion (anyone remember Al Capone).

She was audited and the actual mileage on her car odometer was nowhere near her expensed mileage. There was absolutely no way to explain the situation. Per company policy, she was released. She owed back taxes and a fine from the Internal Revenue Service. Do not let this happen to you. Somewhere there should be a bumper sticker that reads, "Audits Happen".

Foolish deals

The medical and pharmaceutical industries are a microcosm of our society. There are great and honest people as well as dishonest ones. Do not allow short-term gains to skew your thinking process. You have great freedom to make decisions for yourself. In fact, many reps consider their territories as their small business with them as the CEO.

A time will come when an offer is placed before you. If you are a pharmaceutical rep, someone might ask you to buy or sell samples. If you are a medical rep, a distributor might ask you to sell them your trunk stock. We personally heard of a rep's trunk stock being resold all the way to Cuba!

If you get caught participating in one of these "deals," the **best** thing that can happen is you only lose your job. The worst thing could be jail time. That is a high price to pay for a few extra bucks. Never put your family through this. Once you are marked with this type of activity, you will never work in the industry again.

Saying something foolish

Whether you agree or not, political correctness abounds in major pharmaceutical and medical companies. They simply cannot afford to allow insensitivity among their associates. Here is a true example. We were sitting at a table of 12, enduring a corporate awards banquet. A rep who was obviously very attractive won an award and was walking to the stage. As she walked by, one male rep commented, "Look at that."

His career was finished, and he did not know it. A female rep overheard the comment and filed a harassment suit against the company. They did not fire him on the spot, but they made his life so uncomfortable he had to leave.

The competitive nature of this business leads us to believe you can trust only a few people. You never know who is really for you and who is against you. There are many people out there who will bring themselves up by dragging you down. It is best to avoid any conversations that can be viewed as insensitive or demeaning.

"He that would live in peace and at ease must not speak all he knows

or all he sees."

—**Benjamin Franklin**

Doing something foolish

We must always keep our heads in everything we do. Not just in business but in life. The old joke is, "What is the difference between a company car and a Jeep?" Answer: The company car can go anywhere. The following example shows this is not necessarily true.

A rep was moonlighting by selling hotdogs from his company car at the beach. Nothing probably would have come from it had it not taken place during normal business hours! Not only this, but he posed for a picture in the local newspaper. He stood in front of his car at the beach on a Wednesday afternoon with hotdogs in the trunk!

Be constantly aware that everything you do is being watched. When you enter a doctor's office or hospital with a company nametag on, you are associating yourself with your company. You also associate yourself with all coworkers in your territory. (If you happen to work with a less than desirable co-worker, try to distance yourself from that person as much as possible. Try to avoid being in front of the same customers at the same time as well.

Also, do not bring up the co-workers name if you can avoid it.)

Coming up with any answer (lying)

In a perfect world, we would not have to mention this. Our point, however, is a little bit different than what you might be thinking. Your goal is to be thought of as a medical expert regarding your company and your products. Individuals in the medical field will be looking to you as a source of information. This is a good thing.

A problem can arise when a question is posed for which we have no answer. This will eventually happen to you. You can be a new rep or your customer might just be over inquisitive. **Resist giving a response when you do not know the correct answer.**

An intense moment where a rep wants to be viewed as an expert or a patient's well being is at stake can cause anyone to forget this rule. The rep attempts to answer a question when it is obvious to everyone that they do not know the correct answer. Your credibility can be shot. More importantly, the customer might (and probably will) talk about it with others. Now you are losing business due to a bad decision.

It is far better to say, "I do not know, but I know who will." Excuse yourself politely and make a call to your clinical specialist. In most cases, you can get a correct answer to the customer within 10 minutes.

Any insufficiencies that are apparent in your clinical knowledge will be shortly forgotten. You diffused the situation with minimal damage. No one knows everything, so be willing to ask for help.

There is a type of doctor out there (and some arrogant clinical people as well) we want to tell you about. This type of doctor enjoys quizzing reps to the point that they cannot answer their questions. In some regard this is similar to hazing. They are having some fun at your expense. You will know this is happening if they ask you three successive questions.

If you know all the answers, you are in great shape and you should be proud of yourself (buy yourself something as a reward). If you do not, and you realize this is happening, the quicker you say, "I do not know," the sooner it will end.

E-mail and voice mail

As we stated, *not everyone you come in contact with is your friend.* There are people out there who will knowingly hurt you to advance their careers. Be careful of e-mails and voice mails you leave to anyone. As the saying goes, "They can and will be used against you." If you have a problem that must be addressed up the chain of command, consider using voice mail first. A voice message is generally gone when it is deleted. E-mail can be tracked and stored forever.

Speaking of e-mail. Whenever you write a message that goes to anyone, **proofread it thoroughly.** Professional sounding memos and e-mails will improve your image. You never know when an important e-mail you write will be forwarded to upper management.

Absolutely FLY up any Corporate Ladder And Receive Promotion after Promotion

"The only risk of failure is promotion."
—Scott Adams

Now that you have ample information to help you boost sales, what are you going to do with your newfound success? Maybe you can just count your cash. Or you can use your new status to rocket up your corporate ladder.

This brief section is about getting on the inside track within your company. Being on the inside lets you race through one promotion after another, ultimately leading to any job you desire. There are really three keys to know that will propel you quickly through your company. We have simplified them into easy-to-read segments. The results they produce are anything but simple. You can now become that person who literally flies up the corporate ladder.

Find battlefield mentors!

"A single conversation across the table with a wise man is worth a month's study of books."

—Chinese Proverb

Finding a mentor or mentors within your company is critical to moving up the corporate ladder. The bottom line is mega-successful reps have mentors. Normal reps do not. Here is how to find them and use their skill to work the system.

Successful people in all walks of business understand the importance of finding the right mentors. If you have a problem with the word "mentor," use "partner" instead. You should lean on mentors often throughout your career. In fact, lean on them as if your life depended on it. Your sense of urgency (which we discussed earlier), will often dictate what kind of help they give you.

Having the right mentors can help you in the following ways. First, you receive helpful advice from an industry insider. Think of them as a sales coach. You selected them as a mentor because they have information to share. Some companies provide you with one to get started, called a field sales trainer. Spending time with trainers provides ample opportunity for you to judge their abilities. Investigate them fully before making them a permanent mentor. Make sure they have the following:

- great selling skills
- great contacts inside the company
- are well regarded and respected
- have a clean corporate history

If you have selected properly, this is the second benefit. Their inside contacts become yours. In order to advance quickly, you must be familiar with many individuals in the company's home office. Your mentor should help you meet these people. After you meet them, continue a relationship with them. Drop a note just to say hello or ask a question. Keep your name fresh in their heads.

Some companies will not assign anyone to help you. In this case, you must seek out a mentor yourself. Actually, this approach is just fine. Sit back and observe which sales rep the company is most proud of and meets our requirements. Then begin a relationship with that person. Ask to discuss sales strategies, getting in front of doctors or company politics. Tag along on a few sales calls with them. Most people in this industry are proud people. Proud people usually like to share their "wisdom." Remember to ask this person how to advance within the company. They may or may not have good advice. The more input you have, though, the better.

By associating yourself with this top performer, you immediately look better to management. Another golden rule: **Hang out with the top salespeople in the company, and you will become a top salesperson in the company**. At the very least, management will subconsciously associate you with the people they see you with!

Do not limit yourself to one mentor only. There are many people who can help advance your career. Forming a casual acquaintance with many successful reps can only help your situation. Make sure to spend time with these people whenever you are together. At national sales meetings, you will always find the top reps congregating around the bar after the meetings are over. Work your way into these groups and soak up as much information as you can. You will be amazed how helpful this can be.

Find HQ mentors

"Those that will not be counseled can not be helped."

—Benjamin Franklin

Here is step two in getting your "Golden Halo." If you remember, the Golden Halo is the term we use for someone who moves up the corporate ladder with great ease and speed. Many times in our careers, we have looked at someone and said, "How is that person moving up so fast?" Here is the second secret we learned. They had help on the inside *in addition to* great field mentors.

After you find your field mentor, you need additional help from someone inside the home office. Finding that key person in-house can be the difference in moving up in six months, five years or never.

When a co-worker advances rapidly, rest assured that someone in the corporate office gave them assistance. That inside help most likely came from a corporate mentor. Building this type of relationship might be slow or fast depending on your specifics.

If you live in the same city as your corporate office, you should stop by on a routine basis and meet people. It is no secret that reps that live in the home city of a company often get special treatment. Why? There are actually two answers to this question. First, everyone knows them. It is that simple. Simply by being nearby and achieving name-face recognition, relationships are formed. Second, those reps discover who the key opinion leaders are within the company. It is those people we want you to seek out as well.

If you do not live near the home office, the marketing department is usually the best place to start. Begin by establishing a relationship with the people in marketing who handle your products. Call them on the phone, ask them questions and involve them in your projects. Build relationships with as many people as you can this way.

After you understand who the key players are, select the most appropriate one to approach about being your first in-house mentor. The purpose of this step is threefold. First, you want to create an awareness, or buzz, regarding your name at the home office. Second, your mentor can be an inside champion for you and your causes. Additionally, the person provides another set of ears to listen for upcoming opportunities.

Regardless, this section is really about getting help. Here is another tip for after you have identified your prospective mentors. Ask these people *specifically* if they would consider mentoring you. This is paramount with both your HQ mentors and your field mentors. By stating it verbally, you are really asking for a commitment on their part. It is easier to solicit guidance in the future if they already agreed to help you. Do not stop with just one. Fast movers always have multiple mentors and a large number of business contacts! Remember Andrew Carnegic (the world's richest person at the time) constantly surrounded himself with people that could do things he could not. A great model to follow for anyone.

Plan and document your career path

You now have the seeds planted for a personal team to help you reach your desired position. If you want to climb the corporate ladder quickly, you must be willing to look at any opportunity your company presents. Mobility is the key. It may seem unfair, but those people willing to relocate for the best interest of the company are always looked upon most favorably.

That being said, looking for advancement within your company can be a delicate endeavor. You have to play the corporate game. The best way to play that game is with a plan. It is absolutely imperative to sit down with your family and discuss your options and goals. You do not want your career choices to cause a crisis in your home. If you do not discuss your options as a family and come to an agreement, you will pay. We know from experience.

After your family discusses your career possibilities, you must make a decision in one of two ways. First, sit down with your manager and tell them you are willing to accept any job, anywhere that advances your career. Or you can go with option two. This is where you decide in advance only the specific opportunities you would accept. Discuss and document regions you are willing to live in and specific jobs you want. If you choose option two, you must stick to your plan regardless of what other opportunities arise. If you don't, the company will think you do not know what you want. If you switch between option one and two, they would be right.

There are obvious consequences in going with position number two. The biggest of which is your company will not contact you when an opportunity arises outside of your stated criteria. You may not even know those opportunities became available. This can limit your upward movement. For some, the right job is more important than quick, upward mobility. The point of this section is to convince you of the need to make your career decisions upfront.

More Power For Your Trip

The following information is intended to widen the knowledge base for those employees who want to advance their career within the corporation. These are basic strategies for organizing and broadcasting your accomplishments on a résumé and during interviews for promotions.

Keep track of all your wins

You must keep track of all your wins in sales on a current résumé. Being able to brag at the appropriate time is crucial. This is the number one way to impress upper management when promotion time comes around.

Let us illustrate by example. Which of the following people would you choose to interview if you were looking to make a promotion? Mary sells pacemakers with Pete. Their experiences and tenure are about the same. Both have very similar work experiences and patterns of success. Each submits a nice résumé to you. Under their "Experience Section," they have the following information:

Mary

- January 2004 to present. Sales Representative for Electrik pacemakers
- Responsible for selling pacemakers to new and existing customers.

Pete

- January 2004 to present. Sales Representative for Electrik pacemakers
- Responsible for selling pacemakers to new and existing customers.
- Territory started at $100,000 monthly as of January 2004, within six months I grew the monthly revenue to $125,000. A gain of **25 percent** in only six months.

Pete will get the interview over Mary 100 times out of 100 times. Mary may have grown her business to $135,000 monthly. But nobody knows it. As I sit here and read this, **this one piece of information is worth 100 times what this book costs.** Probably a whole lot more. This is also just one example. Imagine if your résumé shows two different ways you grew your sales. What about five ways? Keep building your résumé this way until you have to thin it down. Keep only your best accomplishments.

You would be astonished at how many of our clients send us résumés that look just like Mary's. They pretty much say that, "I have taken up space at XYZ Company for three years." That is it! There is nothing to separate them from the other 100 résumés that a manager might get. This is the single most powerful information you can put on your résumé.

Upper management loves to see numbers. Their entire existence depends on it. In fact, they make money by increasing sales. The more wins you show on your résumé, the more favorably you are viewed. This is true because managers look at sales numbers on a daily basis. Too much in our opinion, but that is another topic.

Keep track of everything that shows you in a positive light! Any congratulatory letter or e-mail or anything positive with your name on it should be filed permanently. Note every single award you won and how you won it. Most sales companies track and post your ranking within the company. Keep these too. If they do not post them, find out where you stand on your own. Someone has this data.

It is also fine if you are not in the nationwide top 10! If you can show that your territory ranking moved from number 50 to number 25, that can be very significant! In fact, we might like to see *that* more than someone who moved from number 10 to number five. Again, try to quantify everything until your résumé is so full you have to cut it back.

Use the awards and letters to build a personal portfolio (or Hero File) separate from your résumé, which will tell any company it cannot live without you. Use this "hero file" when needed. These are great items to pull out during a second interview.

You can even leave a copy of the portfolio of accomplishments and awards with the interviewer. You should personalize the cover page with the manager's name on it. Make copies for other interviewers you talk to as well. Everyone at Vendesi Group kept an updated résumé our entire medical career. You should too.

To the Interview

"Something in human nature causes us to start slacking off at our moment of greatest accomplishment. As you become successful, you will need a great deal of self-discipline not to lose your sense of balance, humility, and commitment."

— H. Ross Perot

A note about safety

In today's environment, your safety is more important than any single job.

Be very cautious about interviewing in hotel rooms. We hate interviews conducted in private hotel rooms, so we do not do it.

If you are asked to interview in a traditional hotel room (where a bed is present and the door is closed), consider asking the interviewer to move the meeting to the lobby or hotel restaurant. You should not be regarded negatively for making this request. If you are, you do not want to work for them anyway. Ultimately you determine the location of your interview; we just want you to be safe.

Appearances can be painful

At the interview stage of the game, the way you look is of vital importance. Research indicates that interviewees are judged *completely* within the first three seconds of the interview. Though you might enjoy dressing hip and having a unique hairstyle, these styles may not be best suited for gaining entry to the medical and pharmaceutical workplace. Employers and customers in this business prefer a conservative appearance.

Your ultimate purpose is to avoid raising any red flags. Remember: **The person conducting the interview has one purpose in mind — find a reason <u>not</u> to hire you.** Enter the room with a nice smile and a firm, but not hard, handshake.

Following our checklist will keep the focus of the interviewer on your accomplishments and not on your appearance. We condensed the following information down to a few lines; so save yourself the cost of a 200-page book on how to dress for an interview. Consider:

Men and Women:

- Wear a dark suit.

- Wear dark colored, polished shoes. (There is a particular interviewer who always pays attention to the cleanliness of a prospect's shoes. He believes if you do not polish your shoes, then you do not really care about his job opportunity.)

- Wear NO cologne or perfumes. It is too hard to measure how much is too much.

- Bring one leather résumé folder with a notepad and pen.

- Bring extra support materials you may need (résumés, reference letters, recommendations or award letters).

Men:

- Wear a white shirt.

- Wear a conservative tie. (A tenured salesman at a men's dress store will have great suggestions for you if you tell him your needs. Remember to bring your suit with you.)

Women:

- Wear a single-colored dress shirt under your suit.

- Steer clear of a scarf during the first interview. We do not believe in trying to stand out with your fashion during a first interview.

For the second interview and beyond, we can relax a bit. By relaxing we mean men can wear a blue shirt with a nice tie, and women can add a scarf or multi-colored shirt if they like. When in doubt, stick with the prior checklist. You will stay out of trouble that way. If you need your clothes to make an interviewer remember you, your résumé is not strong enough.

Core Requirements of Great Interviewing

"Here is the prime condition of success: Concentrate your energy, thought and capital exclusively upon the business in which you are engaged. Having begun on one line, resolve to fight it out on that line, to lead in it, adopt every improvement, have the best machinery, and know the most about it."

— Andrew Carnegie

Regardless if you are moving up your corporate ladder or moving on, there are interviewing essentials every superstar must know. We added this section to make your overall corporate persona as polished as possible. After you have done the hard work described in the last few chapters, you want your interviews to be perfect. The following information on interviewing procedure, questions to be ready for and closing are extremely important.

Before your interview, diligently research the company or new position. You will probably get the following question, "What do you know about my company/new position?" The interviewer is only checking to see if you cared enough to look up some information. If they find that you have not done your background work, you might as well get up and leave. It is over.

This is something we have first hand experience with. A member of Vendesi Group tells a vivid tale of his first interview out of college. He met with a large food manufacturer about a sales position. The interview went along fine for about 15 minutes, then the manager asked, "So, what do you know about my company?" Talk about being stuck! He did exactly zero research on the company. There was no way to wiggle or smooth talk around the question. Not only did he look bad already, but also the manager piled on and imposed the third degree! He began a five-minute rant about how *everyone* he interviews does research on *his* company before their meeting. That was a tough lesson to learn. You get to learn it the easy way – reading it here.

During your research, look for other business units within the corporation. You might discover another opportunity you did not know existed.

Silence really is golden

This is some of the best advice we ever received: After you answer a question, STOP TALKING. Do not say another word until *they* do – even if you sit in silence for 30 seconds or 30 minutes. Some managers will be taking notes so you will want to let them write. Some managers will even pretend to be writing just to see if you can handle the silence. Being comfortable with silence will display your overall comfort level with the process. We would never hire someone who babbled on endlessly after a question was already answered. Some people simply can not stop talking.

It should also be noted that silence *after* a question is asked of you is okay as well. It is better to collect your thoughts for a moment than to rush into a poor answer. This also displays your ability to be thoughtful. You can even turn the tables a bit by using silence against *them* at appropriate times.

Questions to anticipate

We noted earlier, and still believe, that rehearsing 150 questions before you go to interview is not the most effective use of your time. If you follow our process, you will spend more time discussing your accomplishments than answering canned questions. This is always the most desirable position.

However, we do want you to know there are some questions you need to prepare for. Not that you have to memorize an answer, but you will definitely hear something like these, so consider your responses beforehand.

"Tell me about yourself."

This is the first question you will get over 90 percent of the time. It is an easy way for a manager to get the interview going. Running through a quick, chronological list of your experiences is best. Make sure to highlight the top points on your résumé but not every point. You want to make sure they notice all of your major positives and that you get the chance to discuss them later in the interview.

Toward the end of the interview, the interviewing manager will probably ask you if you have any questions. "Tell *me* abou*t you*" is a great question to ask the interviewer. Interviewers' answers will provide insight into their background as well as demonstrate their ability to sell themselves to you.

"Why should I hire you?"

This is Jack Erickson's favorite question. With this question, the interviewer is actually asking you to close the current interview. Most people hate hearing this question, but you should actually love it! You have been prepared!

If you have taken notes (noting the three things that the company is seeking) and matched them to your accomplishments as we discussed, you should be able to give exactly what the interviewer wants to hear.

You might have to think on your feet, but the question affords you the perfect opportunity to link your accomplishments with the company's needs. Take a second to organize your thoughts, then go!

"Where do you need the most improvement?"

It is fine to be honest with your answer here. Try to think of some things in your life you are really trying to improve that don't sound really bad. Something like you try to get too much done at one time is an example of what we are talking about.

Behavioral interviewing

Behavioral interviewing is the current "hot" method used by companies to extract information from you. It is nothing more than asking situational questions about your skills. Think ahead and prepare an example of a time you performed the following:

1. Organization – "Tell me about a time you organized an event."
2. Persuasion – "Tell me how you persuaded someone to an idea of yours."

3. Leadership – "Tell me about a time you took a leadership role. How did it work out?"

4. Teamwork – "Tell me about a time where you worked with a team. How did you accept your given roles?"

5. Relationship building – "Tell me about a time you tried to build a relationship with someone you didn't know."

Consider all the good things **and** the bad things that happened to you while you performed the roles. If there are bad things, remember what you learned from them.

Key Point: *It is okay to make mistakes in your career, just learn something from them.* If you have made a mistake that is brought up in an interview, do not back down from it. Embrace it and promote what you learned. You can do the same thing if you make a big mistake *during* an interview.

Your humility and ability to notice your shortfalls are both important traits!

If you look at each element listed, you see the same thing. They are all <u>Sales Roles.</u> You are selling someone on your point of view, nothing more or less. This is also when you get the "sell-me-this-pen" question. We would like to take a moment on this question because we **love** to get it. The "sell me this pen" question is a huge softball. Here is how we like to answer it.

Don't use this verbatim. Add your own unique style. Begin by asking, "May I hold the pen?" and "Is this the only pen you have?" If they have more, ask them to give them to you for the exercise.

Now ask them to imagine a <u>doctor</u> whose business they have targeted for a long time: They have pulled out every stop trying to get the business but nothing has been successful. The president of your company called and asked why you don't have this doctor's business.

(Hopefully, the interviewer is becoming a bit uneasy.)

Your (the interviewer) cell phone rings, they decided to take your advice and place a huge order. In fact they have five PO numbers for you. What are you going to do? Put them off by asking them to call customer service? Never, you are going to take the POs and call them in yourself! (Start showing the pen) You (the interviewer) might be able to memorize five unique PO numbers. You probably can in fact. But, you might consider this tool my company offers. It will allow you to write on paper all the PO numbers accurately, call in the order, make the sale and be a hero to the president.

After that you could just stop and see what they say. You have done your job and looked great in the process. What you are doing is putting them in a **painful** position. Then you provide a solution to eliminate their pain.

If the interviewer asks what you are doing, simply tell them you are **selling to a customer's pain.**

During the interview, take notes

Be prepared with blank sheets of paper, a pen and Vendesi Group's Interview Manager "Cheat Sheet". Listen diligently for hot button qualifications the manager is looking for and add them to the cheat sheet. If you do not have this cheat sheet, e-mail us at mailto:customerservice@vendesigroup.com and we will send it to you free. When you get the chance to ask a question, ask them specifically, "What are you looking for?" *They should give you at least three items on their wish list.* Write down every one and keep them in mind for later in the interview. You will use this list three times in total.

Prepare for the close of the interview while you are taking these notes. From your point of view, this is the most complex part of the interview process (using our cheat sheet makes the process much easier though.) You must think about two things at once. The first is simply making sure you understand and write down the company's qualifications for the job you are seeking. At the same time, you must be considering how you fit each of these criteria.

Here is a trick-of-the-trade that you will find in no other place. (If you can find this trick published anywhere before us, we will give you your money back for the book!)

- As the interviewer gives you each of the qualifications, write them on the cheat sheet in the qualifications section number's one, two, and three.

- Have a copy of your résumé visible to you.

- Either one by one or after you have all the traits the company is looking for, quickly scan your résumé for the accomplishment that best fits each trait.

- Put the number one by your accomplishment that best matches the first qualification the company wants.

- Do the same for numbers two and three.

- Use this list to indicate to the interviewer how your accomplishments match the company's needs.

Do this right, and you will communicate your abilities better than 99 percent of your competition. Though this concept should be commonplace, only a very few candidates even talk about their qualifications! Even fewer link them to the needs of the company! Doing this comparison effectively proves that you can think on your feet (something you might want to point out)! **You will absolutely shine using this method.** Now you are totally prepared to close.

Closing The Vendesi Group Way

Closing the interview is critical. Mistakes are made and jobs are lost at this point. YOU STILL MUST CLOSE INTERNAL INTERVIEWS. If you fail to "close" the first interview, you probably will not get a second. Closing simply means asking to go to the next step. Even a poor close is better than no close.

When you think the interview is almost complete, the interviewer might ask the following question. "Do you have anything else for me?" or "Do you have any more questions for me?" **This is a request for you to close the interview.** There are many different ways to phrase your close. Use one of these two closing options as a guide.

First Option. If you have not had the opportunity to bridge your abilities with the interviewers' top three hot button traits, you do it here.

- Using the one-two-three system we showed you in the last section, you should be able to effectively connect your positive attributes with the qualifications required of the position. If you already discussed the three traits and how you exemplify them, use the second option.

- If you use the bridge here, it should sound something like this: "I would like to look briefly at a few of the traits you mentioned were needed for this job. The first trait was _____. I have shown my ability to be_____ by doing _____. Second, you said you are looking for_____. I have done this when I _____. Finally you said you needed someone who could _____. I proved I could fill this need in the past when I _____ ____. Based on how my experiences appear to fit your particular needs, is there anything else you need to know before we move forward?"

You will hear a wide variety of answers to this question. You might get a second interview here, but you will probably have to wait. At this point your interview is over, and you have closed it well.

Second Option. If you have already bridged your qualifications with their needs earlier in the interview, move straight to option two. Your author's (Ryan) personal choice is a direct one-liner. I like to ask, "What are your thoughts about me?" It is brief, a bit cocky, and there is no question that I'm closing the interview and putting the ball in their court.

Every time I've used this, the interviewer gives me an honest opinion. Also, you will most likely find out what the rest of the interview process will look like. Some other good closes to try are:

> "What do *we* need to do to go to the next step?"
> "What are your thoughts?"
> "Where do *we* take things from here?"
> "What do I need to do to work for you?"

As a final note, ask the interviewer for the preferred method of follow up. Make sure you get a business card with phone number, e-mail or physical address. Forgetting to get the business card leaves you no way to follow up.

Your follow-up letter

Your follow-up letter should be brief and to the point. This should be the third time you use your interview notes.

- Reiterate the top three qualifications required by the company.

- Bridge their top requirements with your qualifications. Where possible, give specific success stories related to each point. You have now had time to think over your interview so use your strongest traits for each of the three items. Do not be concerned if they are different from the three traits you used during the interview.

- Thank the interviewer for the time and consideration. Say you are looking forward to moving through the interview process.

- Make sure your phone number appears on the letter.

- Try to send this letter out the day of the interview, if possible.

- To garner extra attention to your letter, consider using a service like FedEx or UPS. While this is certainly not necessary, it is impossible to ignore a letter you have to sign for.

More Résumé Power

The basics

We intentionally left off a discussion about the basic elements of a résumé until this point. Few items are unique. Most are standard information for virtually all résumés. We concentrated thus far on building specific accomplishments that pertain to our industry.

You have no choice. Include the required basics in your résumé, but include as much clinical knowledge and as many sales accomplishments as you can.

Your résumé should be a simple, yet effective advertising piece to showcase your skills. There are many effective ways to display information and only a few real rules. Make your best points stand out, and do not be afraid to be bold.

First, follow the one-page rule. Anything more is too much to read.

Second, lead with your strengths. If you are strong clinically, put clinical information first. If your sales accomplishments are superior, make sure they are in the top half of your résumé.

Include the following basic information in your résumé as well:

- Your work experiences
    - o Try to quantify any elements that make you stand out.
- A section on your education
    - o Include any special or unique training or certification.
    - o Include any special recognition or honors.
- List outside groups in which you hold membership
    - o Note any offices you held in these groups.
    - o Describe special events which you organized or in which you participated.

What NOT to do

Unfortunately, lying has become too common in résumés. One of the worst things you can do is lie on your résumé. There are examples left and right about people getting caught falsifying their data. Our society has grown tired of cheaters and liars.

Companies and individuals are currently more likely to prosecute fraud. If you build your résumé with quantified selling experiences and your growing clinical knowledge, you have no need to lie. Your résumé will be superior to your competitors, and you will always come out on top.

"If your résumé can not be trusted, no one will trust you with a $10 million sales territory."

—Ryan Gray

GPA

If your GPA is 3.5 or greater, list it high under your EDUCATION section. If your GPA is not stellar, maybe your Major GPA is better — or your Minor GPA. Make the best choice. Any GPA 3.5 or above should be in bold letters at the top of the section. If it is poor, you might consider leaving it off all together.

Just be ready to discuss it if it comes up. If you follow our résumé-building techniques, this probably will not come up.

Books you have read

This section can be in addition to specific medical reading for a given interview (ex. Journals, white papers, etc.) If your résumé is extra light, listing books you have read might make some sense and give insight to your personality. We would want to see industry books here, not romance novels. Some might include:

The MSDR: Medical Sales Desk Reference™
David Sandler's *You Cannot Teach a Kid to Ride a Bike at a Seminar*
What They Do Not Teach You at Harvard Business School
SPIN Selling
Getting to YES
The Harvard Negotiation Project
How to Win Friends and Influence People
What Customer's Love

Be smart here, use industry, general business or sales titles and make sure you have read anything you mention.

In fact, have one thing you learned from each book ready to discuss with the interviewer. You should have no more than four books listed, so make them count.

Awards you have won

Any awards you have won should be in bold under the section you won them. If you won them as an employee, it should be under that company's heading. If you won it as a student, put it under education, etc. The bottom line is that awards are HUGE things and should be in bold and at the top of their appropriate section. If a large number of people were up for the award, give the number (example: five winners out of 500 contestants). It looks better, and you should know how many people were involved.

Get professional help

If you consider that you might be in a job for 35 to 50 years, the time and money it takes to construct a quality résumé is a fraction of your total effort.

A great résumé that leads to your perfect job can make you EXTRA millions during your working lifetime. Check the personal finance section to see some dollar projections generated with your 401(k) at a medical company. Using the résumé-building section of this piece may be all you need.

If you believe you need more help, consider hiring someone with professional, medical experience to help you put your résumé together. After all, it is the first contact piece that potential employers will see about you. If you are in doubt, e-mail us at mailto:customerservice@vendesigroup.com or another professional medical service.

Well, that is it. Everything you might need to become a great sales rep and create a flourishing career. We also want to say that everything mentioned here is subject to your personality, your style and your abilities. Think of this as sheet music and you are the conductor.

Sign up for our weekly newsletter to receive new and exciting sales tips, industry news and personal-finance information. Go to www.vendesigroup.com to add your name to our list, ask a question or submit a sales idea for cash! We look forward to seeing you there.

Never give up on your dreams. No matter your current situation, anything can be done by individuals who consciously desire and pursue their goals.

"The ultimate measure of a man is not where he stands in moments of comfort and convenience, but where he stands at times of challenge and controversy."
—Martin Luther King Jr.

Appendix – Personal Finance Guide

Overview

- *Max out your 401(k)*
- *If you leave, take your 401(k) with you*
- *Profit sharing*
- *Employee Stock Purchase Plans (ESPP)*
- *Buying stock options*
- *Credit card debt*
- *Your expense reports*
- *The true cost of a car*
- *What you <u>must</u> understand before investing in the market*
- *Make money off your cell phone*

These tips are observations from years of working for medical companies.

The purpose of this bonus section is to **wake you up** and to **get your juices flowing**. If seven-figure bank accounts do not excite you, you are certainly in the wrong business. They sure excite us and we bet this excites you, as well.

If you are already in this business, you have the potential, no the responsibility to be a multi-millionaire in your working lifetime. We believe these jobs also provide the opportunity to give away hundreds of thousands of dollars during your career. Given the plethora of financial opportunities offered by most medical companies, it is easier than ever to create wealth for your family and give money to your causes. Here are some solid ideas that will start you on the path to *generational wealth* for you and your family.

You do not need a 300 page book to instruct you in wealth creation. Just following a few simple guidelines is all it takes. We wish that someone had given us this information when we started!

*** It should be stated that Vendesi Group is neither tax nor investment experts, you should always seek professional help when weighing your options. This section is only a guide to evoke questions to ask your chosen expert.

If you do not think you will ever earn enough money to become a millionaire, think again. If you understand the concept of compounding interest, you will earn it for life. If you do not understand compound interest, you are going to pay it to someone who does. Albert Einstein said that compound interest is the greatest invention of man! Here is how it can work for you. Take a look at only $1 saved a day, compounded daily for sixty-six years at different interest rates.

0%	$24,000
3%	$77,000
5%	$193,000
10%	$2,700,000
15%	$50,000,000
20%	$1,000,000,000

That is ONE BILLION dollars! Think earning twenty percent a year is unheard of? Ever hear of Warren

Buffet? Even if you earn the long term average of twelve to fourteen percent on good growth stock mutual funds, you will be way ahead. Smart medical reps easily stash more into the equation than $365 per year. You should be dropping in much more. If you are earning $75,000 per year, ten percent would be a monthly investment of $625 or $7500 per year, over 20 times our example. Now you can add the following tips and your plan for a personal fortune will be in place.

Max out your 401(k).

When I first began in this business, I was only saving three percent in my company 401(k). The company matched the first three percent, so I thought I would save enough to get the full match (just 3%). What a huge mistake. I needed to save more. 401(k) plans are the easiest road to a couple of million in this business. And they are tax deferred. Simply stated, your deductions are not reported as income to Uncle Sam. Let's use the example of the $75,000 per year earner and use a financial calculator from Kiplinger.com.

Basic assumptions:

Medical rep earning $75,000

$625 (10% of your income) per month into your 401(k)

12% return over 30 years

EQUALS

$ 2,206,196.00 in your 401(k) in 30 years with ZERO company match!

Add in a 3% company match and you end up with

$ 2,868,055 or an additional $600,000 plus!

A six percent company match would change the number to $ 3,529,914.

If you start this process at age 25, you will retire in style by 55.

This is assuming you never earn a raise or sell more products to earn more commissions. If you follow our sales plan, you will earn more in your lifetime than this! In fact, if you are earning $100,000 or more, there is no excuse for not stashing the maximum allowed contribution into your 401(k). **That would be $14,000 in 2005 and**

$15,000 in 2006. If you max today's investment of $15,000 per year with a five percent company match, over a thirty year career your nest egg will grow to $5.8 million. This is in one, individual 401(k) alone!

If you leave, take your 401(k) with you.

401(k) accounts are fully portable if you leave your company. There is one good reason to take them with you that generally trumps any reason to leave them behind. When you leave, you lose control of your account. The company can do things with your money and not tell you about it. It is much safer to roll it over into an IRA or, if you like the fund selection in your new company, you can roll it over to your new company 401(k).

Profit sharing

Not all companies offer profit sharing, but many do. Participation is usually automatic and requires no extra work on your part. Talk to your human resources department about when and if profit sharing kicks in. Some companies add as much as $15,000 per year <u>and more</u> straight into your 401(k) through profit sharing.

Add this to your 401(k) contributions and you are dropping $30,000 per year or more into your account! You can do the math, but we are now nearing EIGHT FIGURES.

Ask about profit sharing when you interview for any position either internal or external. The more information you know about the benefits a company offers, the better your decision will be.

Employee Stock Purchase Plans (ESPP)

Employee stock purchase plans are becoming increasingly popular. Almost all medical companies offer at least some form of these plans. Most of them follow this simple approach. The employee decides to put x amount of money into a plan for a complete year. This money can NOT be touched during this "installment" period. After the year is over, 100% of the money is used to purchase company stock through the plan.

The benefit of the plan is that the purchase price has two possible strike points. You can purchase the stock at the price on day one of the program or day 365 of the program, which ever is LOWER, minus an

ADDITIONAL fifteen percent. This is truly remarkable. Let us look at an example.

On January 1st you begin putting $1000 per month into the ESPP plan.

The stock price of your company is $20 on January 1.

By December 31st you have put $12,000 into the plan.

The stock price of your company is now $24.

On December 31, your company automatically uses all of your $12,000 to purchase stock for the lower of the two stock prices – or $20. Then they take off an additional 15%. So now you purchased the stock for $17. Let's take a look at what you have.

$12,000 / $17 per share + 705 shares

705 shares times the current stock price of $24

EQUALS

$ 16,920 or a net gain of $4,920, a roughly <u>forty</u> percent gain

The greatest thing about this process is not only did you earn forty percent on the money you put in the program in months one and two, you also earned forty percent on the money you put in the program in month twelve!! Try finding a forty percent gain in one month anywhere. They are not easy to come by.

Even if you only earn the fifteen percent the company subtracts from the selling price, these programs are worth their weight in gold. Again, try finding anything else that GUARANTEES a fifteen percent return on your money (some of it in only one month!) Let us know when you do.

Do not think you can part with any additional money? My wife and I were in the same boat and here is what we did. This is another beauty of the plan. If you can make it through the pain of putting money into the ESPP the first year, the rest is cake. After that first year, simply sell the stock from the prior year as you need it for living expenses. Worst case scenario is you use all your prior year's ESPP from year to year. But continue to use the system and you always earn a guaranteed fifteen percent extra bonus on the money you put in. If you can leave it alone, that is great. If not, you are still better off (by fifteen percent minimum) for participating.

Buying stock options

This is a tricky proposition for you. Some companies offer the ability to buy stock options. The payouts can be large, but the risk is large as well. You might never make a profit on your purchased stock options. Take a long look and get some professional advice before venturing off into these waters. Or, just go to Vegas on this one. There are too many great places to put your money. Play this card only if you can afford a total loss.

Eliminate all your credit card debt

This might seem like an odd place to be talking about credit card debt, but it is worth the few moments this will take. Credit card debt is a killer. All the talk we have been doing about compounding interest works in reverse if you have any debt.

The reason we bring it up here is most of us operate our territories with personal credit cards. They might say Corporate Card, but if you are like most of us, the bill comes to you. Do not fall under the misconception your corporate debt is not your personal debt. If you do not believe us, run a credit report and see if the corporate card comes up under your name.

Never use personal debt to finance the company! Make sure every expense you charge will be covered by the company.

Also note. If you work for a company that goes bankrupt, those expenses on your credit card that are work related WILL NOT GET PAID! Cover your self and keep company expenses as low as possible.

Finish your expense reports in a timely manner

YOU CAN NOT AFFORD the hassles that arise when you do not report your expenses in a timely manner. If you get behind on your reports, you will ultimately owe interest, fees and penalties from multiple sources. Some common ones are the credit card company, the cellular phone company, your home phone and long distance carrier, your pager company, and on and on. These expenses generally are all piled on monthly.

Expense reports are a fact of our life. We must deal with them in a timely manner or we ultimately pay the bill.

True cost of a car

There are many companies that offer a car allowance instead of a company car. While these are great perks, they can be a bit tricky to understand exactly how much you really get each month for a car. While these ideas are primarily for those receiving a car allowance, anyone who owns a car can benefit from skimming this section.

Remember the reason we get a car in the first place, we drive an extremely high number of miles in a year. Our cars depreciate faster than a politician's mouth moves. Carefully shifting financial priorities can add thousands of dollars to your net worth over your working career, and they make an immediate impact on your cash flow today.

The first thing to consider is what you <u>really</u> receive from the company for your car. If the company pays you $800 per month for your car, you do not really get $800. The money is taxed as income. So depending on your tax bracket, you receive only $520 true dollars if you are in the thirty-five percent bracket. **Buy your car according to what you are really receiving, not what the company is paying.**

Even when the company tops your car allowance by paying your gas, oil and washes (or decides to pay you some mileage) you are still losing money on your car. Depreciation can be calculated in many ways, but a round, average number is twenty- eight cents per mile. If you drive 30,000 miles in a year, that is $8,400 per year in depreciation on an average vehicle. That is $700 per month for those of you keeping score.

For those of you who want to maximize your dollars spent, buy a car at least a couple of years old and with over 50,000 miles on it. Get one with a good track record of dependability and you can drive it for at least 150,000 more miles. It will always be more cost effective to buy cars this way. Plus you can purchase it outright or pay it off in two years instead of five. Then save your car allowance for the next purchase or pocket it. Either way, you are far ahead of the game.

While I admit freely that I love the fast, German machines, it is probably not your best option - especially if you are not yet in a financially free position. If you have to own one of these beauties, consider buying another car to use for business trips or everyday driving. The money you save by not killing your new 745Li can easily be used to buy a cheap car for day to day business travels.

Have $0 debt (other than your home) before you start investing in the market

This section is talking about managing money outside your 401(k), ESPP, or profit sharing. You MUST maximize all those opportunities first. This section looks at your "play" money you have to invest in personal accounts. You should not start one of these accounts if you have any other debt (other than your house). Instead, use the money you were thinking about investing to pay off your debts. The faster you pay off your debt, the faster you will start truly increasing your net worth.

What really happens when you start investing when you still owe money? Here is a common example that makes our point.

- You owe $15,000 on your cars to XYZ Finance Corp. at eight percent interest
- You have $5,000 invested in the stock market in a liquid account (one that can be sold without penalties) hoping to make a ten percent return.

What you are really doing is borrowing $5,000 from XYZ Finance Corp. to play the market!! No one in their right mind would take out a loan to play the market.

Use that $5,000 to pay down your car. Then continue to pay overpayments if possible to eliminate your debts. Even if you return ten percent profit in a year, you are paying out a guaranteed eight percent to the finance company. That leaves you with a two percent taxable gain with a possibility of losing it all! That is entirely too much risk for a savvy investor. So eliminate your debt as soon as possible.

Make money off your cell phone for you and your company

Long-distance rates are on the rise, so more people are using their cell phones as their primary source of telephone communication. Companies generally pay for your cell phone usage. It is a distinct lifeline between you and your customers. But charging your company $300-$400 a month for a cell phone is too much. You can do better for yourself and for them.

Cell phone companies are forced to be increasingly competitive to get and hold business. By simply making a phone call to check current rates, you might end up making yourself and your company very happy. I will use myself as an example.

I was paying about $250 a month for 1500 anytime, anywhere minutes. My carrier ran a "special" to add a second line to my service. The special was for two lines, 2400 anytime, anywhere minutes (long-distance included) for $115 per month. Let me see, I just picked up 900 minutes I can use to call anywhere, anytime and I have an extra phone line AND the company saves $135 per month. That is a savings of $1620 per year for my company's bottom line, just on *my* cell phone expense. Imagine that multiplied by the 800 reps in the field. No need to imagine, it is over $200,000 in savings per year. Just for sharing this information!

The plan minutes are so high; I never go over the allotted minutes. My home long-distance bill is now about five dollars per month, down from about forty dollars, because I'm using my cell phone for personal long distance.

Everybody wins in this situation. I am sure there are better specials than this available today. Just make a few calls and see if you can save on your home long-distance and a large company expense. If your company balks at your use of your cell phone for personal use, simply point out the numbers and most people will take their savings and move on.

We hope you have enjoyed this bonus information from Vendesi Group! We are excited and honored you read it. Remember, we also cover a wide range of financial topics in our weekly newsletter. Sign up at www.vendesigroup.com to receive this valuable information. Let us know how you are doing, and we will see you at the top.

Best of luck to all!

Vendesi Group Order Form

Additional Copies Available at www.vendesigroup.com

MSDR: Medical Sales Desk Reference – Corporate Edition........................... $29.00

(Group rates are available)

Doctor Trak Software............$34.99

(Group rates are available)

Contact us for speaking engagements, media relations or information toll free at

877.212.0069

Or Contact us via e-mail at

customerservice@vendesigroup.com